SABBATH and SUNDAY among the EARLIEST CHRISTIANS

SABBATH and SUNDAY among the EARLIEST CHRISTIANS

When Was the Day of Public Worship?

SECOND EDITION

David W. T. Brattston

RESOURCE *Publications* • Eugene, Oregon

SABBATH AND SUNDAY AMONG THE EARLIEST CHRISTIANS
When Was the Day of Public Worship?

Copyright © 2017 David W. T. Brattston. All rights reserved. Except for brief quotations in critical publications or reviews, no part of this book may be reproduced in any manner without prior written permission from the publisher. Write: Permissions, Wipf and Stock Publishers, 199 W. 8th Ave., Suite 3, Eugene, OR 97401.

Resource Publications
An Imprint of Wipf and Stock Publishers
199 W. 8th Ave., Suite 3
Eugene, OR 97401

www.wipfandstock.com

PAPERBACK ISBN: 978-1-5326-1861-1
HARDCOVER ISBN: 978-1-4982-4432-9
EBOOK ISBN: 978-1-4982-4431-2

Manufactured in the U.S.A.   MARCH 13, 2017

Earlier, shorter, versions of this booklet appeared

(1) in numbered instalments under title "Sabbath and Sunday" on Examiner.com website; numbers 1 through 9: 8 March 2010 through 31 May 2010; number 10: 18 October 2010; number 11: 10 January 2011

(2) as "Sabbath and Sunday among the First Christians" in *Churchman: A Journal of Anglican Theology* vol. 126 no. 1 Spring 2012, Watford, Herts, England

(3) as "Sabbath and Sunday in Early Christianity" on www.bible.ca website, 2013

Dedicated to my sister,
Kathryn Ann Rayner

Contents

Introduction | ix

1. The Question | 1
2. Unity in Essentials | 3
3. The Lord's Day a Postponed Sabbath? | 7
4. The Sabbath Abolished? | 9
5. Sabbath-Keeping Forbidden | 13
6. The Sabbath Commandment Was Unimportant | 15
7. Luke's Acts of the Apostles 13 and 16 | 17
8. Weekend Observances | 20
9. Every Day Is the Lord's | 24
10. Sources of Information | 27
11. The Hadrianic Persecution | 32
12. The Jewish-Roman War of AD 66–70 | 48
13. Samuele Bacchiocchi | 51
14. Confusion Is Only Apparent | 57
15. Conclusion | 58

Bibliography: The Sources | 61

Introduction

At least since the rise of Seventh Day Baptists in the seventeenth century, there has been disagreement as to the appropriate day of the week for congregational assembly and corporate worship among Christians. The major Saturday-keeping denominations are the Seventh-day Adventists and the multitude of denominations claiming the mantle of Herbert W. Armstrong. This booklet refers to them as "Sabbatarians" because they believe Saturday is to be observed as the main day of both public worship and refraining from secular work, like the Old Testament Sabbath. The Sunday Lord's Day is observed as the chief day of public worship by most other communions in Christendom, some of which rest on this day in the belief they are obeying the Fourth Commandment.

    The present pamphlet, now in its second edition, tries to resolve the differences in convictions, by examining the writings and practices of Christians who flourished so early that there had been no time for deviation from Jesus and the apostles in this regard. Because new Sabbatarian arguments came to my attention after the first edition was printed, this booklet also considers contentions that Christians abandoned the Saturday Sabbath before Constantine, to avoid the Roman government considering them to be Jews, whom they allege the Roman Empire persecuted, with

Introduction

measures including the death penalty. Space is also given to the allegations of the late Rev. Dr. Samuele Bacchiocchi.

This booklet employs only the best evidence of the circumstances it relates, and omits sources that are less than impeccable, even if they advocate Sunday-keeping. For the early period only sources dating from before mass apostasy of AD 249–51 are considered. For the new Sabbatarian allegation that the Roman Empire persecuted Jews, I favor modern authors of the Hebrew faith with access to the most current information.

In choosing such sources of information, I hope to avoid the fallacy of some Sabbatarians in treating every book or article as Holy Writ and of eternal validity, which results in reliance on brief quotations from modern authors as if they possessed the authority and finality of Scripture. Another error that has become too common in Christendom is quoting a sentence or two from any book or article that suits the second writer's purpose, any book or article at all touching on the subject, and treating them as prevailing over the whole of religious literature. They are quoted like proof-texts from Scripture. Good scholarship demands that we weigh the value of any quotation, and also look for context, including whether the author knew any more about the subject matter than the reader.

I hope I am not personally narrowly denominational, close-minded, or unwilling to consider views other than my own. I hope to be ecumenical on a topic-by-topic basis. This has resulted in my articles appearing in journals, magazines, and websites published by members of such denominations as Anglican/Episcopal, Baptist, Christian Reformed, Church of God International (a Herbert W. Armstrong denomination), (non-institutional) Churches of Christ, (non-instrument) Churches of Christ, Congregationalist, Coptic Orthodox, Disciples of Christ, Friends (Quaker), inter-denominational Evangelical, Greek Orthodox, Latter-day Saint (Mormon), Lutheran, Mennonite, Methodist, Moravian, Oriental Orthodox, Pentecostal, Presbyterian, Reformed Churches of New Zealand, Roman Catholic, Seventh-day Adventist, United Church of Canada, United Reformed Church (of Britain), and Uniting Church in Australia.

Introduction

I did not originally set out to write an article or book in favor of Christian public worship specifically on Sunday, or deny that the Saturday Sabbath be so regarded. While compiling my four-volume *Traditional Christian Ethics*, I noticed many scattered references to both Sunday and Sabbath. As a practice run to test the set's viability, I gathered all the entries for Sabbath and Sunday, with the presupposition that I would find a variety of observances and a variety of opinions favoring one day or the other. I had expected to write an essay for some scholarly journal, outlining that some early Christians worshipped on the Saturday Sabbath and others on the Sunday Lord's Day, trace schools of thought, discover relationships in time and geography, and posit surrounding influences to account for why some Christians held public worship on one day, and some on the other. After I had gathered all the references, I was astounded to find that they came out uniform: all the ancients regarded Sunday, not the Sabbath, as the chief day of Christian corporate assembly and worship. Although I rechecked my work, I found the same result held true, with the ambiguous exceptions in Origen's *Homilies on Numbers* and *Homilies on Joshua*, which may be due to alteration of the texts a century and a half later by an editor/translator who had grown up accustomed to Constantine's law making Sunday a day of rest, and suppressing the Saturday Sabbath.

As the facts turned out, I wrote articles and then a booklet advocating modern Christians keep Sunday rather than Saturday. If the facts had been the other way round, this would be a pamphlet in favor of the Saturday/Sabbath as the main day for public worship. Had the results been mixed, the following would be part of an obscure periodical article accounting for differences in days, and you would have never heard of it.

1

The Question

There are strongly-held differences as to whether God wishes Saturday or Sunday to be the main weekly day of Christian assembling and worship. As with many religious issues, both sides appeal to the Bible; then, when arguments based on it fail to convince, they look to the practice of the earliest Christians. For instance, some adherents of a seventh-day Saturday Sabbath allege as fact that Sunday did not become the chief day of the Christian week until the time of the Roman emperor Constantine in the early fourth century AD, when he changed it from Saturday to win over non-Christian sun worshippers.

Consulting early Christian practices and customs is a good idea because they record how Christians lived their faith when the unwritten teachings and Bible interpretations of Christ and the apostles were still fresh in Christian memory, and reveal the consensus of Christian conviction on various matters before they became issues in dispute.[1] These sources also witnessed ways of doing things passed down through overlapping generations.

The present book therefore distils the five hundred (more or less) Christian writings that have come down to us since before the mass apostasy of AD 249–251, in order to determine which day(s)

---

1. E. Flesseman-Van Leer, *Tradition*, 9.

the first heirs of the gospel observed and what kinds of activities God endorsed for the main day(s) of the Christian week.

As in the religious world today, there were differences of outlook even in Christian antiquity as to which day(s) was to be observed, how they were to be observed, whether the Old Testament rules for the Sabbath were still binding, whether Sunday replaced the Saturday Sabbath, and which genres of activities Christians should pursue and which not on the chief day(s) of the week. The present book explores all these issues and will note where there was agreement and where different early Christians practiced different behaviors.

2

Unity in Essentials

The earliest Christian literature, well before Constantine, is unanimous that the main day of the week for early Christians to gather and worship was not the seventh-day Sabbath, but Sunday, which they sometimes called "the first day" or "the eighth day" or "the Lord's Day." We have inklings of this already in apostolic times: (1) in Acts 20.7 Christians at Troas celebrated Holy Communion and listened to a sermon "upon the first day of the week," and (2) in 1 Corinthians 16.2 believers were exhorted: "Upon the first day of the week let every one of you lay by him in store, as God hath prospered him, that there be no gatherings when I come." In opposition to Sabbath-keeping and other Jewish practices, the *Letter of Barnabas* 15. 8–9 speaking from a Christian viewpoint sometime between AD 70 and 132, records that:

> Further, He says to them, "Your new moons and your Sabbaths I cannot endure." Ye perceive how He speaks: Your present Sabbaths are not acceptable to Me, but that is which I have made, [namely this,] when, giving rest to all things, I shall make a beginning of the eighth day, that is, a beginning of another world. Wherefore, also, we keep the eighth day with joyfulness, the day also on

Sabbath and Sunday among the Earliest Christians

> which Jesus rose again from the dead. And when He had manifested Himself, He ascended into the heavens.[1]

Abundant evidence of Sunday as the day of Christian communal worship comes from the middle of the second century. The most replete is in a description of a typical Christian weekly worship service in Justin's *First Apology* 67:

> on the day called Sunday, all who live in cities or in the country gather together to one place, and the memoirs of the apostles or the writings of the prophets are read, as long as time permits; then, when the reader has ceased, the president verbally instructs, and exhorts to the imitation of these good things. Then we all rise together and pray, and, as we before said, when our prayer is ended, bread and wine and water are brought, and the president in like manner offers prayers and thanksgivings. . . . Sunday is the day on which we all hold our common assembly, because it is the first day on which God, having wrought a change in the darkness and matter, made the world; and Jesus Christ our Saviour on the same day rose from the dead.[2]

Justin was a Christian teacher at Rome who was martyred for the Faith around AD 165.

Present-day Sabbatarians deny that "the Lord's day" in Revelation 1.10 indicates Sunday observance, and allege that it was the common term only for the time preceding the Second Coming. However, in *The Epistle of the Apostles* 17, Jesus himself is depicted as calling the eighth day "the Lord's day." Originating in Asia Minor or Egypt in the middle of the second century, this *Epistle* purports to be the revelation of Christ to the apostles. Although we may doubt that it is inspired or scripture or even apostolic, it does witness to an early date for Christians observing Sunday and

---

1. *Letter of Barnabas* 15.8–9, trans. *The Ante-Nicene Fathers*. Edited by Roberts and Donaldson. American reprint ed. by Coxe (hereinafter cited as ANF), 1:147.

2. Justin Martyr, 1 *Apology* 67, ANF 1:186.

describing it as "the Lord's Day."[3] From the eastern Mediterranean, sometime between AD 180 and 200, *The Acts of Peter* begins: "On the first day of the week, that is, on the Lord's day, a multitude gathered together, and they brought unto Peter many sick that he might heal them."[4]

Tertullian had been a prominent lawyer in the City of Rome before converting and being ordained in Tunisia, where he became the founder of Latin Christian literature. He probably wrote *On Idolatry* in his earlier, "catholic" period, when he was a member of the mainline or "Great Church," between AD 198 and the 220s. In Chapter 14, after noting of Christians that "by us, to whom Sabbaths are strange" and mentioning "the Lord's day," Tertullian wrote that it was already well-known by pagans that Christians "have a festive day every eighth day."[5] His earlier *Ad Nationes* 1.13 reminded his readers as a fact similarly well-known among pagans that Christians "make Sunday a day of festivity."[6]

Compiled in Syria, *The Didascalia* is a long comprehensive manual for church practice from the first three decades of the third century. In contrast to Jewish Sabbath customs, the first paragraph of Chapter 21 notes that "on Sundays" Christians rejoice and make good cheer,[7] and in the last paragraph exhorts that all Christians should make good cheer "on the first day of the week."[8]

Bardesan was a Christian scholar who was prominent at the Syrian court before AD 223. He described the unity of Christian behavior and ethics throughout the world. One example he cited was that Christians everywhere assemble on the first day of the week.[9]

---

3. *Epistle of the Apostles* 17, trans. James, *The Apocryphal New Testament*, 491.
4. *Coptic Fragment*, trans. James, 300.
5. Tertullian, *On Idolatry* 14, ANF 3:70.
6. Tertullian, *Ad Nationes* 1.13, ANF 3:123.
7. *Didascalia* 21, trans. Easton, 178.
8. *Didascalia* 21, trans. Easton, 192.
9. Bardesan, *De Fato*, also titled *Book of the Laws of Regions*.

Sabbath and Sunday among the Earliest Christians

While Tertullian wrote more about Christian topics in the Latin language than anyone before Augustine two centuries later, Origen wrote more on them than anyone in any language until Martin Luther thirteen centuries later, after the invention of printing. Origen was the foremost Bible scholar, teacher and preacher of the first half of the third century. Until AD 230 his work centered in Egypt, thereafter in Palestine. Usually half or more of the citations and quotations in my three hundred fifty-odd writings on early Christian behavior and practices come from Origen, due to the larger mass of his writings that have survived. However, the present pamphlet makes relatively little use of him because of the great number of other authors that wrote about the Sabbath and the Lord's Day. His sole contribution as to which is the main weekly day of Christian worship is in *Homilies on Isaiah* 5.2 (sometime between AD 239 and 242). Its best translation is that Christians celebrate the resurrection of the Lord every Sunday, not only once a year or on Saturday.

Thus it is plain that the chief day of the Christian week, even before the middle of the third century, was Sunday. This is evidenced by contemporaneous literature from Troas, Corinth, Egypt, Syria, Rome, Tunisia, and Palestine. There is no extant record of it being on Saturday. In fact, Tertullian's *Apologeticum* 16 makes a direct and unmistakable contrast, using the names of the days that are clear even in translation: "we devote Sun-day to rejoicing, from a far different reason than Sun-worship, we have some resemblance to those of you who devote the day of Saturn to ease and luxury, though they too go far away from Jewish ways."[10]

---

10. Tertullian, *Apologeticum* 16, ANF 3:31.

3

The Lord's Day a Postponed Sabbath?

Was this new Lord's Day merely a one-day adjournment of the old seventh-day Sabbath, for which rest is still mandated? Not according to *Barnabas* 15, the *Acts of Peter*, or Tertullian's *On Idolatry* 14, although Tertullian is not clear in his other treatises. It certainly was not for Ignatius, bishop of Antioch in Syria, who was martyred around AD 107. His *Letter* to the Magnesian Christians 9.1 mentions as common ground between him and them that life in Christ implies "no longer observing the Sabbath, but living in observance of the Lord's Day."[1] Here we see a bishop, writing less than a decade after the death of the last apostle and who doubtless had worked with some apostles, distinguishing between the Jewish Sabbath and the first day of the week as that of Christian worship.

Justin's debate with a Jew uncovers a treasure trove of information about the differences between the two peoples of God in the second century, both from the Christian and from the Jewish point of view. Trypho the Jew faulted Christians of his era because they did not keep the Sabbath, festivals, circumcision, or other Old

---

1. Ignatius, *Letter to the Magnesians* 9.1, ANF 1:62 Shorter Version.

Testament ordinances.² Justin conceded that Christians do not practice circumcision or ritual washings, and even heat water on the seventh day.³ The last-mentioned is still forbidden under Jewish law. Remember that circumcision was one of the crucial differences between the two religions in the Lukan Acts and Paul's letters.

Abounding in statements elaborating differences between Christians and Jews, the *Didascalia*, in whole and in part, is clear that the first day of the week and the Sabbath are not the same.

In the 240s, Origen appeared to have been of the conviction that Sunday is a kind of Sabbath. *Homilies on Numbers* 23.4 favors observing a day of rest—or more precisely, a day of abstinence from worldly activities and temporal affairs—so that Christians will have the leisure to apply themselves more completely to spiritual exercises, such as attending church and listening to the Bible readings and the sermon—activities that other authors describe as usual for the Lord's Day, or first day of the week. Moreover, Origen taught that the Sabbath is but a shadow or symbol of good things to come, as did other ancient Christian writers, e.g. *Didascalia* 26 and Paul in Colossians 2.16f: "16 Let no man therefore judge you in meat, or in drink, or in respect of an holyday, or of the new moon, or of the sabbath days: 17 Which are a shadow of things to come; but the body is of Christ."

More clearly, in AD 249 or 250, Origen preached that a distinctive mark of Christians is that they do observe the Sabbath, but not by resting from the enjoyments of everyday life but only from indulging in sin.⁴

---

2. "[Y]ou, professing to be pious, and supposing yourselves better than others, are not in any particular separated from them, and do not alter your mode of living from the nations, in that you observe no festivals or sabbaths, and do not have the rite of circumcision; and further, resting your hopes on a man that was crucified, you yet expect to obtain some good thing from God, while you do not obey His commandments." (Trypho in Justin, *Dialogue* 10, ANF 1:199).

3. "Is there any other matter, my friends, in which we are blamed, than this, that we live not after the law, and are not circumcised in the flesh as your forefathers were, and do not observe sabbaths as you do?" (Justin *Dialogue* 10, ANF 1:199);"Be not offended at, or reproach us with, the bodily uncircumcision with which God has created us; and think it not strange that we drink hot water on the Sabbaths." (Justin, *Dialogue* 29, ANF 1:209).

4. Origen, *Homilies on Joshua* 2.1.

4

The Sabbath Abolished?

With three dissenting voices, Christian authors before the mass apostasy of AD 249–251 believed that Jesus abolished the Sabbath completely. According to *The Acts of Peter* in the late second century, Christians in the City of Rome "had in mind also how that Paul had oftentimes contended with the doctors of the Jews and confuted them, saying: Christ, upon whom your fathers laid hands, abolished their sabbaths and fasts and holy-days and circumcision, and the doctrines of men and the rest of the traditions he did abolish."[1]

The same is implied in Justin's *Dialogue with Trypho* 10. In the late second century or early third century, the *Letter to Diognetus* 4.1 characterized the Jewish concerns for sabbaths and circumcision as "utterly ridiculous," "unworthy of notice," and "superstition."[2] Some scholars attribute this *Letter* to a former tutor of the Roman emperor Marcus Aurelius (AD 121–180). The *Didascalia* 26 speaks of Christ "fulfilling" the Sabbath, which therefore need no longer be observed.

In his catholic period, Tertullian's *Answer to the Jews* 2.10 taught that the Sabbath and circumcision were not valid for all

1. *Acts of Peter* 1 Vercelli manuscript, in James 304.
2. *Letter to Diognetus* 4.1, ANF 1:26.

Sabbath and Sunday among the Earliest Christians

time and all peoples, but were confined to Jews under the Law of Moses and were abolished for the Christian (the present) dispensation. Chapter 4.1 is bolder: "the Sabbath is demonstrated to have been temporary"[3] and opines that any references to it in Christian Scriptures denote the permanent rest at the end of time, a common belief among early Christian writers. In the 220s Origen wrote that all Christians believe that neither circumcision nor Sabbath rest nor animal sacrifices in the Bible are to be understood literally nor practiced since the time of Jesus.[4] In *Homilies on Genesis* 5.5 Origen dismissively preached that "there is nothing great" in observing circumcision and the Sabbath.[5] The *Didascalia* 26 also denied that the Saturday Sabbath has any validity or binding force outside the period from Moses to Jesus, and ridiculed the custom of being idle one whole day in seven.

Although obscure, there was support for the belief that Sabbath obligations continue for Christians, in a highly modified way that probably applied to weekdays as well. In his *Letter to Flora* in the middle of the second century, the Gnostic Ptolemy discussed the various components of divine law and said that God wants us to keep the Sabbath by refraining from doing evil, and to fast in the sense of abstaining from sin.[6] God has not so much abolished the Sabbath, wrote Ptolemy, as transformed it. He added that even Christians (or his sect of them) observe "the external practice of fasting,"[7] providing it is done for the proper motives,[8] but mentioned no similar provision for abstaining from work on the Sabbath. Another Gnostic book, the famous *Gospel of Thomas* 27, in the second half of the second century or earlier, also exhorted to

---

3. Tertullian, *Answer* 4.1, ANF 3:155.

4. Origen, *De Principiis* 2.7.2.

5. Origen, *Homilies on Genesis* 5.5 trans. Heine in *Origen: Homilies on Genesis and Exodus*, 118.

6. Ptolemy, *Letter* 5.12.

7. Ptolemy, *Letter* 5.13 trans. Froehlich in *Biblical Interpretation in the Early Church*, 41.

8. Ptolemy, *Letter* 5.13.

"fast as to the world" and "keep the Sabbath as Sabbath,"[9] but is unclear as to whether this fasting is only from sin and as to whether this Sabbath is on the first or seventh day of the week. There is no context to help tease out a clearer meaning or how this Sabbath is to be kept, because the *Gospel of Thomas* consists only of random short isolated sayings unconnected to those next to them.

Marcion held doctrines similar to the Gnostics, the most important of which was that there is one god of the Old Testament and a totally different god of Jesus and the New Testament. The two deities are in conflict with each other and require different kinds of behaviors from people. One argument Marcion employed in support of this doctrine was that the god of the Old Testament commands Sabbath observance while that of the New does not. Here we have an enemy of mainstream Christianity seizing on a difference as well-established. To prove that there is only one deity, Tertullian's *Against Marcion* defended the continuity of the Bible and its God. As for the Sabbath, Tertullian said that Christ did not rescind, annul or destroy it, although confining its prohibitions to human works for one's own benefit as distinct from work he would permit for healing, restoring, and other "divine" work. He would also permit preparing meals, and preserving body, health, and life on this day. He defended the Sabbath as "a day which is to be free from gloom rather than from work."[10]

As he gradually drifted away from mainstream Christianity, Tertullian moved more and more towards the rigors of Sabbath-keeping, as can be expected from the general strictness of the cult he later joined. His early *Answer to the Jews* 4 speaks of the Sabbath, like circumcision, as having been a merely temporary provision, binding only in the Mosaic age, and is not nor should not be devoted to the resting that Moses had commanded: "we Christians understand that we still more ought to observe a sabbath from all 'servile work' always, and not only every seventh day, but through

---

9. *Gospel of Thomas* 27 trans. Blatz in *New Testament Apocrypha*, ed. by Schneemelcher trans. Wilson, rev. ed., 1:121.

10. Tertullian, *Against Marcion* 4.12, ANF 3:363.

all time."[11] Almost as early, his *On Idolatry* 14 states that to Christians "Sabbaths are strange."[12]

"Christ did not at all rescind the Sabbath" and "He did not utterly destroy it"[13] asserts his later *Against Marcion* 4.12, which denies that Jesus annulled it, although Tertullian still maintained the proper way of observing it to be different from that in pharisaic-rabbinic Judaism. For instance, Tertullian wrote that it is to be "free from gloom rather than free from work."[14] Yet *On Fasting* 15 unmistakably indicated that the Sabbath and the Lord's Day are two separate days of the week, on neither of which may Christians fast. However, this does not necessitate all sabbath-keeping, for *On Fasting* deals only with various forms and rules of fasting. Discussion as to which is the day of public worship would be off-topic.

About AD 233 Origen preached that the gospel allowed "work on the Sabbath, except work for profit" on the same principle that it permits "food, unless it is spoiled."[15] One of the marks of Christians, said Origen (as mentioned above), was that they observe the Sabbath, not in the sense of resting from everyday life, but resting from sin.[16]

---

11. Tertullian, *Answer to the Jews* 4, ANF 3:155.
12. Tertullian, *On Idolatry* 14, ANF 3:70.
13. Tertullian, *Against Marcion* 4.12, ANF 3:363.
14. Tertullian, *Against Marcion* 4.12, ANF 3:363.
15. Origen, *Homilies on Luke* Rauer's Fragment 107, trans. Lienhard, 171.
16. Origen, *Homilies on Joshua* 2.1.

5

Sabbath-Keeping Forbidden

Some authors actually prohibited Sabbath-keeping. Justin wrote that it was not the practice of the Great Church—the majority, mainstream Christians—to be circumcised or to observe the Sabbath or other Jewish institutions, but added that they were practiced by sectarians who warped the true faith. He considered it a sin for them to try to persuade other Christians to keep the seventh-day Sabbath.[1] In a less ecumenical age than our own, Tertullian forbade any attendance of Christians at pagan or Jewish festivities or observing their holidays. Keep the eighth day, he said, but not the Sabbath—which he described as alien to Christians.[2]

Commenting about the Sabbath, *Didascalia* 26 proclaims: "every day is the Lord's, for the Scripture says 'The earth is the Lord's and the fullness thereof: the world and they that dwell therein.'"[3] In his defense of the Faith against pagan taunts, Origen in the late 240s replied:

> we ourselves are accustomed to observe certain days, as for example, the Lord's day, the Preparation, the Passover, or Pentecost. I have to answer, that to the perfect

1. Justin, *Dialogue* 47.
2. Tertullian, *On Idolatry* 14.
3. *Didascalia* 26, trans. Connolly, 236.

Christian, who is ever in his thoughts, words, and deeds serving his natural Lord, God the Word, all his days are the Lord's, and he is always keeping the Lord's day.[4]

Was "the Preparation" the new Christian name for the old Jewish Sabbath? In *Homilies on Exodus* 7.5 Origen indicated that it was Friday, the sixth day, that Christians called "the Day of Preparation" while the Sabbath is the seventh day, which he clearly distinguished from the Lord's Day. In the AD 190s, Origen's predecessor as the dean of the world's most prominent institution of Christian education, wrote that the seventh day is to be a day of rest or "abstraction from ills—preparing for the Primal Day."[5] The context is ambiguous as to whether this Primal Day is the Lord's Day that follows every Sabbath or the era of our reward at the end of time. Mark 15.42 and Luke 23.54 corroborate that "the Preparation" was the day before the Sabbath.

---

4. Origen, *Against Celsus* 8.22, ANF 4:647.

5. Clement of Alexandria, *Stromata* 6.16, ANF 2:512 The Fourth Commandment.

6

The Sabbath Commandment Was Unimportant

Before the devastating epidemic and mass apostasy of A.D. 249 to 251, Christians regarded the Fourth Commandment as unimportant, and perhaps no longer binding under the New Covenant. This is the injunction in the Ten Commandments to remember the Sabbath day and keep it holy. When Christians in this foundational period recited or summarized the Ten or gave examples of its contents, they always, always, omitted the Fourth one.

Sometimes early Christians partially enumerated the Ten Commandments as still binding, sometimes as good rules of conduct evident from nature in human beings, sometimes as binding only on Jews, and sometimes as proof of what a wise and beneficent lawgiver God is. Although in some instances the Christians were quoting from memory, the omission of the Sabbath also occurs in works that originated only in writing, with the author possessing the luxury of suspending his activity to research a point or ascertain the exact wording of Scripture. Whether the form was originally oral or written, early Christian sources consistently omitted the Sabbath when summarizing or giving examples of God's law.

How many Commandments were recited, and which ones, varied from author to author and book to book. Most of them included the prohibitions against murder, theft and adultery. These are the only ones cited by Bishop Hippolytus in his early-third-century *Refutation of All Heresies* 5.15. Idolatry is also included in Romans 2.21–22, in Clement of Alexandria,[1] and in Theophilus, who was bishop of Antioch in the third quarter of the second century.[2] Theophilus and Romans 13.9 detail the commandment against coveting also. False witness was included in the list as forbidden, and honoring one's mother and father as mandatory in the AD 180s by Bishop Irenaeus in France,[3] who was the teacher of Hippolytus, by Clement of Alexandria, by Theophilus, and in Origen's *On First Principles* 4.19 and *Commentary on Romans* 2.9.1, all of which originated in writing. Origen's other mentions are in *Commentary on Romans* 9.31.1 in writing, and *Homilies on Numbers* 11.1.8 in oral preaching. All speakers and writers, from Jesus to Origen, omitted the Sabbath commandment as part of Christian law.

The only exception, a Christian listing or summary that included the Sabbath, was Tertullian's *On Modesty* 5. This was in a violent attack against the orthodox, mainstream, church after he had joined a narrow, rigorous, sect.

Jesus himself was notorious to the scribes and Pharisees for what they considered nonchalance about the Sabbath. His attitude is illustrated in Matthew 19.18–19, Mark 10.19 and Luke 18.20. Mark and Luke record Christ as beginning with "Thou knowest the commandments" and enumerating murder, theft, adultery, honor to parents, and false witness. Like the Apostle Paul, and his other followers for two centuries, Jesus omitted the Sabbath. Thus, even "the Lord of the Sabbath" considered it as not immediate in mind when listing the Ten, or not correctly applied by the Pharisees and other Jews.

---

1. Clement of Alexandria, *Paedagogus* 3.12.
2. Theophilus, *To Autolycus* 5.15.
3. Irenaeus, *Against Heresies* 4.12.5; AD 180s.

7

Luke's Acts of the Apostles 13 and 16

In support of their position that the Saturday Sabbath, rather than Sunday, was the main day of Christian assembly and worship until the fourth century, sabbatarians cite the thirteenth, sixteenth, and eighteenth chapters of the Lukan Acts, which narrate that the Apostle Paul and his companions attended synagogue and preached on Sabbaths. When asked to preach again in Acts 13.42 and 44, they did not do so the next day (Sunday) but on the following Sabbath. The sabbatarian interpretation goes that Christian preaching, and therefore the main Christian community assembly to hear the word of God and worship, was on the Sabbath, not Sunday.

The relevant verses quoted for this position are:

Acts 13.14: "they came to Antioch in Pisidia, and went into the synagogue on the Sabbath day, and sat down."

Acts 13.42: "And when the Jews were gone out of the synagogue, the Gentiles besought that these words might be preached to them the next Sabbath. 44 And the next Sabbath day came almost the whole city together to hear the word of God."

Acts 16.12: "And from thence to Philippi, which is the chief city of that part of Macedonia, and a colony: and we were in that city abiding certain days. 13 And on the Sabbath we went out of the city by a river side, where prayer was wont to be made; and we sat down, and spake unto the women which resorted thither."

Acts 18.4: "And he reasoned in the synagogue every Sabbath, and persuaded the Jews and the Greeks."

However, a more plausible interpretation is that the apostolic company went to the synagogue on the Sabbath because it was when they would have the largest audience. The Saturday Sabbath was and is the main day for Jews to assemble and listen to readings from the Law of Moses and the prophets (Acts 13:15; 15:21). In this they were joined by "God-fearers," who were Gentiles that were attracted by Jewish (and later Christian) ethics and belief in a single deity, but were not ready to formally convert to Judaism.[1] Other examples are in Luke 7.2–5 and Acts 10.2, 7, 22. Do not forget that visitors at synagogue were often requested to preach on the readings (Acts 13:15), which provided a splendid opportunity for evangelization uncommon elsewhere or on other days of the week. Paul and company attended for this extraneous reason, not out of any Christian obligation to worship on that day or among Jews. Remember also that in predominantly Gentile milieus Paul preached in the marketplace also, and at a sort of Hyde Park for discussion of metaphysical subjects (Acts 17:16–21), yet sabbatarians do not oblige anyone to preach in these venues today.

The apostles did not partake in synagogue rites as passive worshippers in the pews. Acts 17.17 records that Paul "disputed" in a synagogue, and 13.45 that the apostolic preaching and teaching there resulted in envy, blasphemy, and contradicting on the part of their hosts. What the apostles intended was not Sabbath-keeping as a pious obligation, but to utilize a ready-made a forum for evangelizing.

If Paul would not evangelize Jews and Gentiles on any day but the Sabbath, did he suspend his mission on Sundays and weekdays? Acts 20:7 indicates not.

---

1. Becker, 572; Eliav, 579; Fredriksen, 592, 595–597.

It is also to be observed that, in Canada at least, the main television series that advances this sabbatarian argument (*Tomorrow's World*) is broadcast on Sunday, not Saturday. The motive for the choice of day is the same: to approach potential converts on the day they think most about religion, and are most receptive to messages about it.

8

Weekend Observances

So far, we have established that the Sabbath (Saturday) and the Lord's Day (Sunday) are different in concept from each other in the Christian week. Christian literature before the mass apostasy of AD 249–251 reveals that—despite the unity of ancient sources on this issue—they differed as to how the two days are to be observed, with each having its own behavioral precepts as to what believers should do on the respective days.

Among Christian authors before the middle of the third century there was a variety of attitudes on how to keep the Sabbath or Lord's Day, sometimes both. Activities mandatory or encouraged for Sunday, the Lord's Day, included attending church. This was inculcated by many early authors,[1] such as Chapter 14.1 of the *Didache*, a church manual written when many apostles were alive, and probably before the Gospel of Matthew. The entire fourteenth chapter is instructive and informative:

> Chapter 14. But every Lord's day gather yourselves together, and break bread, and give thanksgiving after having confessed your transgressions, that your sacrifice may be pure. But let no one who is at variance with his fellow come together with you, until they be reconciled,

---

1. Acts 20.7–11; Justin, 1 *Apology* 67; Bardesan; *Didascalia* 13.

that your sacrifice may not be profaned. For this is that which was spoken by the Lord: "In every place and time offer to me a pure sacrifice; for I am a great King, says the Lord, and my name is wonderful among the nations."[2]

Except for *Didascalia* 13, the same sources contemplated that Holy Communion would be held there every Sunday. Acts 20, Justin 1 *Apology* 67, and *Didascalia* 13 included listening to the Bible readings and sermons there. *The Didache* 14 would add the confession of sins before Communion. Paul and Justin recorded contributing to the relief of less fortunate Christians as a regular Sunday activity (1 Corinthians 16.2, 1 *Apology* 67). Christians should be joyful on the Lord's Day, according to *Barnabas* 15.9, Tertullian *Apologeticum* 16 (as distinct from the observance of Saturn-day, "we devote Sun-day to rejoicing"[3]), and *Didascalia* 21. Curiously, *Didascalia* 21 exhorts to both fear and trembling and also good cheer on the same day. Uncharacteristically short of words, Origen had nothing to say about Christian duties for Sunday except to celebrate the Resurrection,[4] and wanted believers to strive at (1) self-control of the body on the Lord's Day, and (2) "abstaining from the pleasures of this life which lead astray so many."[5]

The Didascalia was against idleness on the Lord's Day, and also idolatry, attendance at pagan assemblies, the theatre, fairs and festivals for idols, as well as absenting oneself from a Christian assembly and using worldly business as an excuse for not attending it,[6] levity, telling jokes, singing pagan songs, afflicting oneself, and (again) pagan assemblies.[7]

There was general agreement that the Lord's Day is a day for worship, not an unstructured holiday for recreation and doing whatever one liked.

2. *Didache* Chapter 14, ANF 7:381 under title *The Teaching of the Twelve Apostles*.
3. Tertullian, *Apologeticum* 16, ANF 3:31.
4. Origen, *Homilies on Isaiah* 5.2.
5. Origen, *Against Celsus* 8.22, ANF 4:647.
6. *Didascalia* 13.
7. *Didascalia* 21.

Sabbath and Sunday among the Earliest Christians

Barnabas 15.6f states that the Sabbath is observed by sanctifying oneself, purity of heart, and "properly resting,"[8] which only lead to other questions. More particularized are Ptolemy *Letter to Flora* 5.12, which mandates resting from sin, and Clement *Stromata* 6.16, which prescribes resting from "abstraction of ills"[9] in preparation for the Lord's Day the next day. Tertullian would permit religious functions, healing, preserving, saving life, doing good, gentleness, mercy, and working for the benefit of any soul.[10] Origen would have Christians attend church each Sabbath, listen to the Bible readings and sermon there, meditate on heavenly things and on the Day of Judgment, and other spiritual exercises,[11] and abstain from the work of sin.[12] He would permit working, but not for profit.[13]

Origen's lack of particulars for Sunday observance and his contrasting abundance of details for the Sabbath led me to the speculation either that he considered or treated the Lord's Day like a Sabbath, or that he meant "Sunday" when he said "the Sabbath." For instance, he prescribed attendance at church and listening to the Scripture readings and sermon for Saturday,[14] but he made no such provision for Sunday, which six authors before him indicated was the main weekly day of Christian assemblies for public worship, and he himself had stated was the day Christians commemorate Jesus' resurrection.

For almost two years I puzzled over the anomaly of Origen contradicting all other authors before AD 251 and his own *Homilies on Isaiah*. The best I could do for the first print publication of this piece was to ask readers to email me if they had the answer.[15] Over a year later, I remembered that we do not possess the origi-

8. *Letter of Barnabas* 15.6, ANF 1:147.
9. Clement, *Stromata* 6.16, ANF 2:512 The Fourth Commandment.
10. Tertullian, *Against Marcion* 4.12.
11. Origen, *Homilies on Numbers* 23.4.1.
12. Origen, *Homilies on Joshua* 2.1.
13. Origen, *Homilies on Luke* Rauer's Fragment, trans. Lienhard, 107.
14. Origen, *Homilies on Numbers* 23.4.1.
15. *The Churchman* 126, no. 1 (Spring 2012):30.

nal texts of *Homilies on Numbers* or *Homilies on Joshua* in pristine form but only in Latin translations dating from the turn of the fifth century by a churchman named Rufinus. He translated many of Origen's writings and is noted for condensing, interpolating into, and "correcting" them, in his belief that he was updating them, highlighting their accord with the doctrine of the church in his day, and deleting or altering what he believed were insertions or corruptions by heretics during the intervening century and a half, or more. Thus, the exact wording of the two sets of homilies better represent the conditions of the late fourth and early fifth century than the first half of the third.

Even so, Tertullian had indicated that, even in his day, it was a pagan practice to take Sunday as a holiday, which would indicate that Constantine merely conferred official status on an existing heathen custom:

> It is you, at all events, who have even admitted the sun into the calendar of the week; and you have selected its day, in preference to the preceding day as the most suitable in the week for either an entire abstinence from the bath, or for its postponement until the evening, or for taking rest and for banqueting.... you who reproach us with the sun and Sunday should consider your proximity to us. We are not far off from your Saturn and your days of rest.[16]

This also bolsters the evidence that Sunday was the main day of the Christian week as early as the late second century.

---

16. Tertullian, *Ad Nationes* 1.13, ANF 3:123.

9

Every Day Is the Lord's

In practice, the distinction in early Christian times was not as broad as in our secularized world today. Compiled in 217, Hippolytus' *The Apostolic Tradition* 35.1f assumes that local congregations hold services—especially Bible study, instruction and prayer—every morning of the week in order to equip Christians to withstand the trials of the day. A bishop in central Italy and once a rival bishop of Rome, Hippolytus produced this book not as exhibiting his original ideas but to codify existing church practice as it had descended from the apostles. Good Christians attended these services every day of the week (36.1), thus rendering weekends less of a contrast than in our culture. Remember also from Origen that Christians also observed Fridays, called "the Preparation." Indeed, Acts 2.46–47 narrates of the earliest Jerusalem Christians, "And they, continuing daily with one accord in the temple, and breaking bread from house to house, did eat their meat with gladness and singleness of heart, Praising God, and having favour with all the people."

With the ambiguous exception of Origen, all Christian writers that commented about weekends prior to the middle of the third century agreed that Christians are to hold our main assemblies and celebration on Sunday, the first day of the week. They were divided about the seventh-day Sabbath, with a variety of opinions and practices for Saturday. Contrary to an unwarranted assumption in modern times, keeping both the Sabbath and the Lord's Day are not mutually exclusive in concept, nor does the chief day on which public worship is held necessarily have to coincide with the day of rest. Equating the two is purely jumping to a conclusion not shared by the first practitioners of the gospel. The author(s) of *The Didascalia* certainly envisioned, even commanded, that secular work be performed on the day for public worship. Chapter 13, titled "An Instruction to the People to be Constant in Assembling in the Church," mandated "whenever you are not in the Church, devote yourselves to your work; so that in all the conduct of your life you may either be occupied in the things of the Lord or engaged upon your work, and may never be idle."[1] It also forbids using a heavy workload as an excuse for not attending church, which indicates that it accepted that Christians work on this day. Although it is true that Sunday did not become a day of mandatory rest until Christianity was co-opted into the state apparatus in the fourth century, it is also true that it—and not the Saturday Sabbath—was the chief day of Christian gathering, worship, and Holy Communion from apostolic times.

Except for Tertullian's later, heretical, writings, there was a liberal or tolerant attitude as to the separation and respective modes of observing (or not observing) the Sabbath and Lord's Day. In discussing differences in practice arising from matters of principle between groups within a congregation, Romans 14.5f in the middle of the first century dismissed the matter as indifferent: "One man esteemeth one day above another: another esteemeth every day alike. Let every man be fully persuaded in his own mind. He that regardeth the day regardeth it unto the Lord: and he that regardeth not the day, to the Lord he doth not regard it." In Galatians 4.9 to 11, Paul expressed alarm that local Christians were reverting to their previous Judaic observances, from which he said Christ had liberated them. Paul negatively criticized these believers because "Ye observe days, and months, and times, and

---

1. *Didascalia* 13, trans. Connolly, 129.

years" (v. 10), which Paul considered contrary to the pure gospel. Colossians 2.16 witnesses to a mechanism for enforcing this indifferentist principle: "Let no man therefore judge you in meat, or in drink, or in respect of an holyday, or of the new moon, or of the sabbath days."

10

Sources of Information

It is not enough to flatly state that early Christians held their main public worship on Saturday or only on Sunday. The onus is on the proponents of one view or another to quote or cite early sources, just as this book does for ancient Sunday as the day of worship. In Christianity today, too many people allege that an apostolic or other early state of affairs had existed, without substantiation from original contemporary sources. All teaching and practice must be affirmatively proved from the best evidence available. Otherwise, any sort of statement can be made about anything, and that which can prove anything proves nothing.

    Nor is a nineteenth- or twentieth-century Bible commentary or declaration an admissible source of evidence. Because long-lost documents from ancient Christian times are being discovered every two decades or so, we in the twenty-first century know more about the earliest period than did the near-modern commentators. Not even fourth- and fifth-century church historians are reliable when they tender opinions on earlier Christian practices unless they actually excerpt from the documents written during the period under discussion.

Sabbath and Sunday among the Earliest Christians

For instance, there are three reasons why the church histories of Socrates Scholasticus and Sozomen[1] cannot be regarded as valid evidence for our subject:

(1) they both wrote in the fifth century, hundreds of years after the period described in the present pamphlet. By contrast, the above cites only sources contemporaneous with the people and practices they describe

(2) they both began their accounts with the Emperor Constantine, and did not specifically address themselves to what happened seventy-five to three hundred years before his time. They did not cover the same period as the present booklet, and

(3) in the two references favored by Sabbatarians, they were not describing ordinary weekly worship, but the diversity and local customs in different places in observing Lent, especially the week immediately before Easter Sunday. They were not writing about what happened outside Holy Week. From the opening decades of the third century, Tertullian *On Fasting* 14, Hippolytus *Apostolic Tradition* 29, and *Didascalia* 21 attest that different rules for the Sabbath and Lord's Day applied to this season, as distinct from those governing ordinary weekends, as is still the case in many denominations today.

Nor is it enough to extract many "suggestions" from different places in Scripture that tangentially touch on a practice, and then lay supposed implication upon supposed implication, when there is clear evidence in contemporaneous or near-contemporaneous Christian writings. The best possible information is obtained when ancient authors are writing specifically on the topic of Christian weekly worship rather than brushing against it when discussing an unrelated topic.

Much has been written, and is still being written, on the authority by which the Sabbath was changed to Sunday, as many

---

1. Socrates Scholasticus, *Ecclesiastical History* 5:22; Sozomen, *Ecclesiastical History* 7:19.

authors imagine to be the case. Such modern-day writers assume, without evidence from the Bible or earliest church, that the main day for the Christian public assembly and worship is necessarily the same as the Sabbath, which they assert was the situation before the fourth century.

Proponents for Saturday public worship overmuch rely on statements pronounced in the nineteenth and early twentieth centuries on the topic of the church of the first three centuries. One problem here is that many important Christian documents dating from before AD 249–251 were not discovered until late in the nineteenth century, and some not until the twentieth. Because these resources were not available to them, such statements have been superseded by those in the late twentieth or twenty-first centuries, such as those which this pamphlet uses.

Sabbatarian authors rely heavily on Roman Catholic propagandists such as James Cardinal Gibbons (1834–1921), Archbishop of Baltimore. The thrust of such Roman Catholic literature is that there is no scriptural warrant for the transfer of the Sabbath to the first day of the week but is valid and binding only because Jesus gave the Roman Church wide-reaching authority to alter Biblical precepts and to introduce or change doctrines and practices in addition to the Bible, or even in contradiction of it. It was the Roman Church, wrote the proponents of the papacy, that changed the day to the practice now followed by most Protestants (indeed, most Christians). The papal argument ran that if Protestants accept one Roman innovation, they are logically compelled to accept them all, and thus yield to the pope in all other matters, abandoning their doctrine of the sufficiency of Scripture. Stated alternatively, Gibbons and his confreres asserted that if a Protestant accepts the practice of the Church of Rome when it altered one of the Ten Commandments, he/she must accept all Roman beliefs and practices.

There are three fallacies in the Sabbatarian reliance on such Roman Catholic literature. First, it assumes that the Roman Church has always been incorrect in every detail; whatever Rome does is automatically bad. A more reasonable sentiment is that religious truth is not an indivisible whole, and that the pope is sometimes correct when other Christians share a practice. Second, such Sabbatarian literature uses scare tactics dating from a time when popery was regarded as a malign conspiracy bent on destroying human rights, patriotism, and common decency. The Christian is duty-bound, implied the Sabbatarians, to oppose and be unlike Rome in as many ways as possible, even when this entailed discarding the practices of the early Christians. Third, such Roman Catholic literature is best described as "triumphalist." It was not written as a balanced presentation of uncontroverted history, but as propaganda to win Protestants into full formal membership in the papal church through arguments built on logical consistency; it was directed to Protestants who did not know the reasons for their beliefs and practices and lacked the resources to learn about them.

The Roman Catholic contentions were themselves flawed. First of all, there was no pope or bishop of Rome until the middle of the second century. The New Testament envisions congregations being led by more than one official, synonymously termed "bishops," "elders," or "presbyters." It was not until the beginning of the second century that one of them began to be set apart, and designated as the sole "bishop" separate from the committee of elders. This change did not occur everywhere at once. Starting in Syria, it spread westward only gradually, and did not reach the City of Rome until mid-century. Even *The First Letter of Clement*, written in the City on church government in the second half of the first century, knew only committees of elders/presbyters. Second, whether led by a single bishop or a committee, it was technologically and organizationally impossible for the church of the City to enforce innovations or compliance over the whole of Christendom, even though mostly confined to the Mediterranean world. Communications were too sporadic and undeveloped. Any long journey was time-consuming and hazardous; that of Saint Paul in Acts 27 and 28 was not unusual. Travel was even more dangerous when the church was persecuted, with any papal emissaries, had they existed, being stopped or killed en route.

Sources of Information

Third, uncontroverted contemporaneous facts indicate that the early centuries knew nothing of the present Roman Catholic system of religious governance and supremacy. Bishop Irenaeus of France and most bishops in western Turkey felt free to argue with the bishop of the City in the late second century, and the eastern bishops steadfastly continued for centuries a practice objectionable to the pope of Rome. A similar controversy raged in the AD 250s between the pope on the one side and bishops in Turkey and a large host of north African bishops on the other. These incidents would have been inconceivable if it were part of early Christian belief that the papacy divinely held authority to make modifications within the Faith, let alone alter Biblical commands such as a seventh-day Sabbath.

Fourth, evidence of Sunday observance was too widespread and is attested far too early to have been enacted by the bishop of Rome. Even if we dismiss Justin Martyr as a witness because he wrote in the City when it had a solo bishop, there remain the attestations in Troas, Corinth, Egypt, Syria, and Palestine, and also in Tunisia by Tertullian, who opposed papal claims to oversight over the worldwide church.

While there was scope for individual liberty or variations among believers as to exact details of how the Saturday Sabbath and Sunday Lord's Day are to be observed, the best available sources were unanimous that the Old Testament Sabbath and the Christian Lord's Day are not the same, and that the Lord's Day rather than the seventh-day Sabbath is the approved day for Christians to assemble and worship as a church.

11

The Hadrianic Persecution

The evidence that Christians kept Sunday rather than the Saturday Sabbath before Constantine in the fourth century AD has become so overwhelming that some Sabbatarians acknowledge that some Christians before his era worshipped on the Lord's Day, Sunday. However, these Sabbatarians argue that the change to Sunday began as a result of persecution of the Jews under the Roman Emperor Hadrian during and after the Bar Kokhba Revolt, rather than from apostolic times. Others would place it just after the suppression of the Jewish revolt in AD 70.

To drive the Romans out of the Jewish homeland, re-establish an independent state, and rebuild the Temple, the Jews of Jerusalem and Judea revolted against the rule of the Emperor Hadrian from AD 132 to 135. The war was marked by fierce fighting, heavy casualties, and atrocities on both sides. Christians did not take part. After the Revolt was suppressed, Hadrian turned Judea into a thoroughly gentile region by expelling the Jews, rebuilding Jerusalem as a pagan city, and severely restricting Jewish access to it and the surrounding countryside. In an attempt to preclude further Jewish uprisings, cripple Judean identity, and end Jewish attachment to their part of Palestine, many Jewish religious practices were prohibited, with people that continued them being punished, sometimes

The Hadrianic Persecution

by death. The new Sabbatarian argument continues that, in order to escape persecution as Jews, Christians changed their day of worship to Sunday to distance themselves from them in government eyes. These Sabbatarians are correct that the Revolt and Hadrianic Persecution were important in widening the differences between the two religions, but there is no evidence from this time period that Sunday services did not begin until so late a date.

The attempt to backdate the change by a hundred and ninety years before Constantine, and identify the Hadrianic Persecution as the cause, is a "could have been" which requires solid proof, from the best evidence by people reporting from the relevant time period, or we will need to adopt chapters 2 through 9 of the present pamphlet, which demonstrate that Sunday worship dates from the time of the apostles, if not earlier.

To determine the validity of the new Sabbatarian thesis, we must examine (1) whether the Roman government had previously distinguished between Christians and Jews, for the purpose of persecution, (2) which Jewish practices Hadrian or his lieutenants outlawed that would affect Christians, (3) how reliable are the Jewish sources about the extent and categories of prohibited actions, (4) whether the Persecution affected only Judea or was Empire-wide, and (5) whether Hadrian's persecution lasted long enough for Christians to become uniform in implementing Sunday as their main day of assembly and worship.

The present pamphlet prefers ancient contemporary and near-contemporary sources as more accurate than nineteenth- and twentieth-century commentaries on them, because they were closer to the people involved. Some Sabbatarians often cite the eleventh edition of the *Encyclopaedia Britannica* in support of their ideas about the Sabbath, but neglect to mention that it was published in AD 1911, which means it is now over a century out of date. The *Catholic Encyclopedia* is of similar vintage. Alexander Hislop, author of *The Two Babylons*, which they like to cite, died in 1865. Philip Schaff, the author of another of their favorites, *History of the Christian Church*, passed in 1893. These publications could not incorporate developments in scholarship and research after they were published, such as that coming from numismatics, archaeology, and more recent manuscript discoveries.

Where evidence from ancient times is deficient, I supplement it with later treatises of our own day, with a preference for scholars of the Jewish faith, as being more likely to present the case most favorable to depicting Roman suppression as thoroughgoing, oppressive, and wide-ranging, and therefore more supportive of the view that Christians might be tempted to change their main weekly day of worship to escape the strictures on Jews.

1. The Roman government before AD 135 already distinguished between Judaism and Christianity as separate religions.

Because it did, there was no need for Christians under Hadrian to distance themselves by giving up worship on Saturday.

According to Gedaliah Alon, a modern Jewish scholar published by the Hebrew University of Jerusalem, the Romans persecuted Christians "steadily and relentlessly" before the time of Constantine, but Judaism was protected.[1] Since the time of Julius Caesar, Roman law tolerated Judaism because it was a religion continuously practiced since ancient times. What Romans could not tolerate was new religions, ones that could not prove they had been practiced since antiquity. According to the prominent Jewish scholar Martin Goodman, Christians were punished for not participating in the worship of Roman gods, from which Jews were legally exempt, and were persecuted on their own account, not for any connection with Judaism.[2]

In AD 64, the Emperor Nero clearly distinguished Christians from Jews when singling out and executing the former after the Great Fire. The *Annals* of Tacitus (AD 56 to 117) refers to the victims as following a religion which was "a mischievous

---

1. Alon, *Jews in their Land*, 635.
2. Goodman, *Rome and Jerusalem*, 488.

The Hadrianic Persecution

superstition," "hideous," and "shameful,"[3] which harbored "hatred against mankind."[4] Writing of Nero, Suetonius in the time of Hadrian narrated "Punishment was inflicted on the Christians, a class of men given to a new and mischievous superstition."[5] Jews were not included in this persecution.

As shown by the correspondence around AD 112 between a pagan Roman governor of Bithynia and the Emperor Trajan, Hadrian's immediately predecessor, the fact of being a Christian was not only a capital offence, but Imperial officials actively sought out all Christians in their province.[6] The Jews were unmolested.

Hadrian was emperor from AD 117 to 138. Early in his reign, two Christian writers independently presented him with detailed descriptions of their religion. The one we possess in full described at length the differences between Christianity and the older religion.[7]

Before the Revolt, Hadrian had set out rules for detecting and trying Christians as criminals in his *Rescript to Caius Minucius Fundanus*, proconsul of Asia. It clearly regards Christianity as outlawed in itself, and different from Judaism, which was legal. Hadrian wrote the *Rescript* around AD 125—about ten years before anti-Jewish decrees related to the Bar-Kokhba Revolt.[8]

In the reign of Antoninus Pius (reigned AD 138 to 161), the next emperor after Hadrian, the government regarded the Jews with such favor around AD 155 that they were prominent in the execution of the Christian bishop of Smyrna,[9] and influenced the Roman governor to burn his body so completely that Christians would not be able to treasure his relics.[10] Also during this reign, Ptolemaeus

---

3. Tacitus, *Annals* 15.44.2–8, trans. Church and Broadribb, 304.
4. Ibid., 305.
5. Suetonius, *Twelve Caesars* Nero 6.16.
6. Pliny the Younger, *Letter to Trajan* 10.96; Trajan *Reply to Pliny* 10.97.
7. Aristides, *Apology* 2, 14, and 15.
8. Hadrian, *Rescript to Minucius Fundanus*, ANF 1:186.
9. *Martyrdom of Polycarp* 13.1.
10. *Martyrdom of Polycarp* 17.1–18.1.

and Lucius were martyred on the sole charge of being Christians.[11] These incidents indicate both that Christianity was outlawed, on pain of death, and that Judaism was held in government favor.

The next emperor, but one, after Hadrian, was Marcus Aurelius (reigned AD 161 to 180). He was a philosopher-emperor, deeply interested in philosophy and dedicated to the material and spiritual welfare of his people.[12] Considering Christianity to be a threat to them, he reiterated the law that Christians be put to death.[13] For example, Justin Martyr and six fellow-Christians were beheaded as a group for confessing their faith and refusing to sacrifice to Roman deities.[14] Justin had previously written that Gentiles generally put people to death solely for confessing to be Christians.[15] Marcus considered Christians to be obstinate, defective in judgment, and fit only to be executed; he considered them to act without dignity and put on too much of a show when being killed.[16] Although considering Jews to be habitually dirty in body and rebellious in spirit,[17] he maintained government toleration of them.

Sometime between AD 185 and 190, the government acted on a Jewish complaint by punishing a Christian who had created a disturbance in a synagogue on a Saturday Sabbath. Both the complaint and government action would have been impossible if Judaism were illegal. Indeed, the prosecuting Jews reminded the judge: "Romans have conceded to us the privilege of publicly reading those laws of ours that have been handed down from our fathers."[18]

Around AD 200, Tertullian wrote of Jews as a viable and functioning community, although in dispersion from their homeland.[19] According to an ancient document discovered in 1902, they

11. Justin, *2 Apology* 2; Eusebius, *Church History*, 4.17.9, 12–13.
12. McHugh, "Marcus Aurelius," 570.
13. Eusebius, *Church History* 5.1.47.
14. *Martyrdom of Justin and Companions* 3–5.
15. Justin, *Dialogue with Trypho* 96.
16. Marcus Aurelius, *Meditations* 11.3.
17. Ammianus Marcellinus, *Roman History* 22.5.5.
18. Hippolytus, *Philosophumena* 9.7, ANF 5:129.
19. Tertullian, *Answer to the Jews*, 13.

The Hadrianic Persecution

were accorded the status of Roman citizens in AD 212,[20] which the New Testament indicates had been reserved to very few people in the time of the Apostle Paul.

In contrast, Christians were subject to ever-worsening Empire-wide persecutions until the reign of the Emperor Constantine in the early fourth century. Because of the protected status of one religion and the unfavorable treatment of the other, Christians from AD 138 to 313 were not tempted to maximize differences between themselves and the older religion in government eyes by meeting on Sunday instead of Saturday and be subject to milder treatment.

As summarized by Professor Goodman in commenting on the difference between Jews and Christians in Roman eyes, "it is clear that those officials who punished Christians did not see them as any sort of Jew."[21]

2. Which Jewish practices were outlawed?

This is an important question if the Romans forbade activities that Christians shared with Jews, and the Persecution would thus prohibited aspects of the Christian faith. It also raises the issue of how severely Roman law restricted the exercise of the two religions.

As a preferred contemporary or near-contemporary Jewish source, we will look first at the Talmud. A commentary on the Torah (Old Testament) and a record of the oral law (Mishnah) and rabbinic discussions of them and application to the changed circumstances in which they lived, it consists of reports of conversations among Middle Eastern rabbis in the first centuries AD. There are two Talmuds: the Jerusalem Talmud and the longer Babylonian Talmud. The present book cites only the latter because of difficulties with translation. According to Sacha Stern, Schwab's French translation of the Jerusalem version is "very unreliable," that of Neusner "eccentric and unsatisfactory."[22] My personal command of the French

---

20. *Constitutio Antoniniana de Civitate*; Strack, and Stemberger, *Talmud and Midrash*, 3; Schwartz, "Ancient Jewish Social Relations," 551.
21. Goodman, *Rome and Jerusalem*, 488.
22. Stern, "Talmud Yerushalmi," 150.

language is insufficient to read the tortuous and convoluted style which characterizes the Talmud. Nor can I locate texts in Schwab or Neusner from the citations of modern-day commentators. Guggenheimer's (which Stern characterizes as "problematic")[23] and Artscroll's English translations were incomplete when I looked.

Because it uses the Talmud's mode of interpreting the Old Testament and dates from the same eras, I include the Midrash under the general designation of "Talmud."

The (Babylonian) Talmud alleges that the following were forbidden after the Bar-Kokhba Revolt: circumcision,[24] observing the Sabbath,[25] ordaining a rabbi,[26] studying the Torah,[27] observing the Torah,[28] abstaining from sex with a menstruating woman,[29] unleavened bread in the Passover season,[30] abstaining from shaving the head,[31] possessing a palm frond on Succoth,[32] phylacteries,[33] prayer shawls,[34] adjusting the Jewish calendar to fit with the seasons,[35] religious assemblies,[36] and possession of a Torah scroll.[37] Most of these were of no interest to Christians anyway.

Other strictures against Jewish practices have been extracted from the Talmud by modern scholars who possess a greater facility

---

23. Ibid.

24. Rosh Hashannah 19a; Me'ilah 17a, Baba Bathra 60b, Leviticus Midrash Rabbah 32.1, Psalms Midrash Book 1 Psalm 12.5.

25. Berakoth 61b; Rosh Hashannah 19a; Me'ilah 17a; Leviticus Midrash Rabbah 4.32.1; Psalms Midrash Book 1 Psalm 12.5.

26. Sanhedrin 14a; Abodah Zara 8b.

27. Berakoth 61b; Rosh Hashannah 19a; Abodah Zara 18a.

28. Berakoth 61b; Baba Bathra 60b.

29. Me'ilah 17a.

30. Leviticus Midrash Rabbah 32.1; Psalms Midrash Book 1 Psalm 12.5.

31. Lamentations Midrash Rabbah 5.5.

32. Leviticus Midrash Rabbah 32.1.

33. Ibid.

34. Ibid.

35. Sanhedrin 12a.

36. Berakoth 61b; Abodah Zara 18a.

37. Abodah Zara 18a.

The Hadrianic Persecution

than I with Jewish and Roman literature of the second century AD. Ra'anan Abusch states that ritual ablutions were banned during the Hadrianic Persecution.[38] In a long, apparently exhaustive, list at pages 94 to 97 of "Persecutions and Martyrdom in Hadrian's Days," Moshe David Herr[39] includes among government prohibitions: ritual immersion,[40] gifts to priests and Levites, kindling Hanukkah lights, the Sabbatical year, Jewish arbitration tribunals, public reading of the Book of Esther, and reciting the Shema, and relates that the Romans demanded forced labor on the Sabbath.[41]

Yet, even the material most favorable to the Sabbatarian argument indicates that identifying oneself as Jewish, and professing the Hebrew religion, were not in themselves forbidden. The Talmud records that Hadrian was on speaking terms with Jews and interacted with them on a one-to-one basis without persecuting them, unless they acted against the government in another manner. There were rabbis at Hadrian's court.[42] The Emperor even counseled a gentile who wished to convert of Judaism.[43]

Although Jerusalem and its environs may have otherwise been barred to Jews and other circumcised men,[44] they were permitted to visit the ruins of the Temple annually, on the ninth day of the Hebrew month Ab.[45] One Ph.D. in ancient Mediterranean religions specifically contradicts Eusebius, saying that the ban on Jews entering Jerusalem "could not have been easily enforced, and rabbinic tradition knows nothing about it."[46] Rome continued to collect the head tax on Jews, at a heavier rate than on gentiles.[47] These two dem-

---

38. Abusch, "Negotiating the Difference," 81.
39. Herr, "Persecutions and Martyrdom," 94–97.
40. Ibid., 94–97, 101.
41. Ibid., 101
42. Chagigah 5b; Genesis Midrash Rabbah 10.3, 13.9, 28.3, 78.1.
43. Exodus Midrash Rabbah 30.12.
44. Sandgren, *Vines Intertwined*, 334; Schäfer, *Jews in Antiquity*, 159.
45. Schäfer, *Jews in Antiquity*, 164; Smallwood, *Jews under Roman Rule*, 460.
46. Sandgren, *VinesIintertwined*, 276.
47. Appian, *Roman History: Syrian Wars*, 2.11.8.50; Leaney, *Jewish and*

onstrate that neither Jewish religion nor identity were illegal. In fact, Jews were free to combine to form a lobby, without molestation, for the repeal of the strictures upon their people.[48]

3. How reliable are the Talmudic accounts?

The Talmud was not written all at once, nor by a single author. It is not a contemporary account by people who themselves lived under the Hadrianic Persecution. It originated orally, consisting mostly of discussions among rabbis, and was passed on orally for decades or centuries. At each retelling, parts of it were subject to what Moshe Lavee describes as "a varied degree of creative redaction and flexible transmission."[49] Throughout the transmission process, new generations adjusted the content and context to be more understandable in their own times. Indeed, the purpose of the discussions was to adapt the gist the Torah, the Mishnah, and earlier parts of the Talmud, to the changed circumstances of later ages, which often obscures access to the original material.[50] According to Professor Goodman, "their stories accreted more and more legendary elements over time."[51] Doctor Smallwood describes the situation as "the whole tradition of the persecution is no more than an elaboration of the single pre-war prohibition on circumcision," which "could readily be regarded as magnified into a prohibition of the practice of Judaism as a whole."[52] Even when opining that "a substratum of truth must underlie the tradition," she admits that we have to make allowance for "substantial exaggeration and distortion."[53]

Christian World, 125; *Psalms Midrash* Book 1 Psalms 12.1; Origen, *Letter to Africanus* 14; Sandgren, *Vines Intertwined*, 334; Suetonius, *Twelve Caesars* Domitian, 8.12.

48. Rosh Hashannah 19a; Me'ilah 17a.
49. Lavee, "Rabbinic Literature," 325.
50. Ibid., 325; Kalmin, "Problems," 169.
51. Goodman, *Rome and Jerusalem*, 465.
52. Smallwood, *Jews under Roman Rule*, 465.
53. Ibid., 466.

The Hadrianic Persecution

The prominent Jewish author and editor, Peter Schäfer, finds it improbable that there was a comprehensive, systematic persecution, even in Palestine by itself.[54] He notes of the alleged prohibitions as to Torah study, the Sabbath, and other Jewish religious practices: "the further away the sources are in time from the historical event of the Bar Kochba revolt, the more extreme the persecution becomes."[55] The rabbis, he writes, gradually blew up a ban on circumcision "into a systematic and massive persecution of the Jews."[56]

The above quotations and paraphrases are from reputable scholars in Judaica. Less authoritative is the characterization by a professor of visual and performing arts, who has at least authored biographies of the Romans Cicero and Augustus Caesar. He describes the relevant rabbinic allegations as "hysterical sources,"[57] "if we can trust Talmudic tales,"[58] and "hyperbolic rabbinical tradition."[59]

Although holding that there is substance in the Talmudic accounts of the anti-Jewish legislation, Moshe David Herr states that many were "extremely difficult to enforce full compliance."[60] I myself wonder how the government could enforce the law to engage in sex with a menstruating woman. Enforcement was so difficult and lax that a common evasion was to allege that the action in question was neutral, without religious significance.[61] An example is dissembling that an immersion in water was not baptism or religious purification ritual but a common, everyday bath.[62] Rabbis counseled obeying the Roman laws outwardly, and dissembling

---

54. Schäfer, *Jews in Antiquity*, 159.
55. Ibid., 160.
56. Ibid.
57. Everitt, *Hadrian and the Triumph*, 302.
58. Ibid., 303.
59. Ibid., 304.
60. Herr, "Persecutions and Martyrdom," 102.
61. Ibid., 102, 111.
62. Ibid., 102.

about the nature of their actions.[63] They even held that, to save one's life, a Jew could disobey any precept of the Torah, except those against murder, incest/adultery, and idolatry.[64] Christianity had always forbidden these to its adherents, but they posed a problem: the Romans did not command Jews to worship idols,[65] because they had been exempted when Judaism was legalized over a century earlier. Not so with Christians. The government occasionally demanded that everyone within its borders sacrifice to the Roman deities and emperors, as a sign of patriotism and supplicating the gods to continue the welfare of the Empire. The usual reason Christians were persecuted was that they refused to do this, considering it to be unfaithfulness to God and worship only Him. It would have been in the Christians' interest to seek to be regarded as Jews, and to corporately worship on Saturday, unless the Sunday commandment had long been integral to their faith.

4. The geographical extent of the Hadrianic Persecution

For all Christians to decide to change their day of public worship, the Hadrianic Persecution must have been worldwide, or at least Empire-wide. There would be no point for Christians outside the zone of persecution to make the change, for they could worship freely on the Saturday Sabbath.

The first indication that the Persecution was not universal is provided by modern scholars of the Hebrew faith. Moshe David Herr notes that the ban on circumcisions "was enacted only to apply to the province of Judea and not to the rest of the Empire."[66] Gedaliah Alon opines that the Romans did not try to obliterate Judaism as such, for they did not apply the strictures to the Diaspora.[67] David Goodblatt and Aharon Oppenheiner indicate that the

63. Ibid., 109.
64. Sanhedrin 74a; Herr, "Persecutions and Martyrdom," 108; Smallwood, *Jews under Roman Rule*, 474.
65. Herr, "Persecutions and Martyrdom," 99.
66. Ibid., 93 n. 27.
67. Alon, *Jews in their Land*, 636.

The Hadrianic Persecution

Persecution did not extend to Galilee.[68] Professor Oppenheimer further writes that "Babylonia acted as a magnet for refugees from the Bar Kokhba Revolt,"[69] and that there were "Waves of refugees" to Galilee and Babylonia.[70]

Even religious leaders could escape the Persecution simply by moving out of Judea. A rabbi illegally ordained there fled to Asia Minor, which indicates that the Persecution did not extend that far, even though part of the Roman Empire.[71] Many Judean rabbis found full religious freedom by moving to Babylonia, where there was a large, thriving Jewish community which had been self-governing since the first century AD.[72]

Another line of evidence reveals that local authorities possessed jurisdiction to repeal and reinstate decrees about the Sabbath and circumcision in their areas of governance.[73] According to one Jewish scholar, "the emperor himself was probably not involved in the specific prohibitions (except for the ban on circumcision)."[74] Ra'anan Abusch denies that Hadrian ever forbade circumcision, much less in the Diaspora.[75] Sandgren thinks "Even the postwar ban on circumcision may have been issued not by Hadrian but on a local level by Tineius Rufus, governor of Judaea during the revolt."[76] Under Roman law, the inhabitants of Judea were a conquered people rather than law-abiding Roman subjects, and as such the local governor possessed the authority to deprive them, as he saw fit, of any religio-cultural activities they formerly possessed. By the same token, his restrictions did not apply to areas

---

68. Goodblatt, "From History to Story," 176; Oppenheimer, "Attempt of Hananiah," 256.

69. Oppenheimer, "Attempt of Hananiah," [255].

70. Ibid., 256.

71. Baba Metzia 84a, p. 83 n. 1.

72. Strack, *Talmud and Midrash*, 3, 83; Oppenheimer, "Attempt of Hananiah," [255].

73. Me'ilah 17a.

74. Alon, *Jews in their Land*, 646.

75. Abusch, "Negotiating the Difference," 73.

76. Sandgren, *Vines Intertwined*, 273.

outside his province, such as Galilee and the Diaspora.⁷⁷ Smallwood attributes the responsibility to Sextus Julius Severus, who succeeded Tineius Rufus.⁷⁸ The status of being a conquered people seldom lasted long.⁷⁹

5. How long did the "Hadrianic" Persecution last?

Whatever the activities forbidden or commanded, the geographical extent, or Hadrian's part in it, the Persecution did not last long. Beginning with the suppression of the Bar-Kokhba Revolt in AD 135, it continued only until Hadrian's death in AD 138—hardly enough time for Christians throughout the world or the Empire to deliberate and decide to change their main weekly day of public worship. There is abundant evidence that the anti-Jewish decrees were soon repealed by Antoninus Pius (reigned 138 to 161), his successor as emperor.⁸⁰

When circumcision became legal for Jews once more, there was little point to retaining the other prohibitions.⁸¹ For example, a group of them was allowed to reside in Jerusalem.⁸² Systematic and Empire-wide persecution of the Jews as a faith group did not begin until the Emperor Constantine.

Circumcision as an example

Scholars still debate whether Hadrian outlawed circumcision before or after the Bar-Kokhba Revolt, i.e. whether the prohibition was a cause or result of it. He did not criminalize all aspects of Judaism or persecute all Jews on account of their religion; he merely

---

77. Alon, *Jews in their Land*, 636.
78. Smallwood, *Jews under Roman Rule*, p. 463 n. 138.
79. Alon, *Jews in their Land*, 636.
80. e.g. Shabbat 33b; Rosh Hashannah 19a; Smallwood *Jews under Roman Rule*, 470–72.
81. Smallwood, *Jews under Roman Rule*, 472.
82. Schäfer, *History of the Jews*, 164.

The Hadrianic Persecution

forbade circumcision, as earlier and later emperors had done, e.g. Domitian (reigned AD 81–96) and Nerva (reigned 96–98). Graeco-Roman aversion to circumcision was not based on religious grounds, but because society regarded it as unnecessary surgery, and cruel, barbaric, and disfiguring. The last-mentioned was far more important and noticeable than today, because the Greeks and upper-class Romans held their sports in the nude and glorified the complete human body.[83] Even the rector of Christianity's foremost institution of learning between AD 192 and 202 recommended that Christian men should wrestle in the nude for health purposes.[84] Jews and other practitioners of circumcision merely got in the way of the majority ethos.

The letters of the Apostle Paul reveal that there were widespread discussions, even arguments, about who in the local church was circumcised, and who not. How did one Christian know the state of another's penis? It was because they constantly saw each other bathing, which was more common than sports. In Roman times, only the wealthiest possessed bathing facilities in their homes.[85] Even they, along with everyone else, usually washed in large public pools, which were often the venue of local community life, totally in the altogether.[86]

Public nakedness in the baths was so commonplace that the *Didascalia* in particular exhorts Christian men and women not to bathe (nude) in front of the opposite sex,[87] and women to wash only at the hours pools were reserved for females.[88] Around AD 249, the bishop of Carthage thought it necessary to remind nuns of this.[89] Bathhouses were maintained in every Roman community, urban and rural, large and small, no matter how long they might

---

83. Toner, *Leisure and Ancient Rome*, 50–51.
84. Clement of Alexandria, *Paedagogus* 3.10.
85. Fagan, "Socializing at the Baths,'" 358.
86. Fagan, "Leisure," 382; Toner, *Leisure and Ancient Rome*, 54–55.
87. *Didascalia* 2–3.
88. *Didascalia* 3.
89. Cyprian, *Dress of Virgins* 19.

be in use.[90] The Talmud mentions that the Romans built bathhouses in Judaea.[91]

So strict are modern Jewish rules on bodily modesty that persons knowledgeable about medieval Jewry, or about the ultra-orthodox in our own day, can hardly conceive of Jewish nudity at public baths. Yet, according to an Assistant Professor of Rabbinic Studies and Jewish History, "not only did Jews visit the bathhouse regularly, they also lauded its benefits and partook of its cultural proceedings."[92] They also shared other aspects of Roman culture that are now forbidden in the Jewish tradition.[93] He accounts for the difference by pointing out that in the first and second centuries AD Jewish law was still rudimentary, incomplete, and flexible, and did not possess the luxuriance of rules that has characterized it since the Middle Ages, for the Talmud and other Jewish legal pronouncements were still in the process of being developed and elaborated. Rabbinic sages were still extending rule upon rule upon rule and extension upon extension upon extension in building a fence around the Torah and around the Talmud itself, but this came only after the historical period discussed by the present pamphlet. In any event, Roman Jews desirous of appearing naked in public could cite the precepts and examples of the prophets (1 Samuel 19.24; Isaiah 20.2–4; Micah 1.8).

Some men sought to conceal their circumcision by wearing a sheath in the vital location, but it could often fall off inopportunely.[94]

After Hadrian's death, removal of foreskins was permitted to Jews,[95] some of whom had disregarded the ban even before it.[96] Antoninus, the new emperor, permitted only Jews to circumcise;

---

90. Fagan, "Leisure," 380; Fagan, "Socializing at the Baths," [358], 363, 368; Yegül, *Bathing* 155.

91. Shabbat 33b; Toner, *Leisure and Ancient Rome*,.

92. Eliav "Jews and Judaism," 579.

93. Ibid.

94. Martial, *Epigrams* 7.82.

95. Leaney, *Jewish and Christian World*, 467.

96. Smallwood, *Jews under Roman Rule*, 471.

The Hadrianic Persecution

it remained forbidden to all other peoples.[97] The only other exceptions were priests of the Egyptian religion, to whom it was also a faith-based rite, and permitted only after enquiries of the candidate by secular and religious officials.[98]

In the *Dialogue* with Justin Martyr before the middle of the second century, the Jew Trypho insisted that, to obtain God's mercy, a man must first be circumcised and keep the Sabbath.[99] The Christian Justin specifically rejected this contention.[100] Justin remarked that removal of the foreskin was what separated Jews from Christians and all other peoples.[101] Neither debater spoke of it as contrary to secular law, or performed in secret.[102]

For Christians, circumcision was optional, but for Jewish males it was a badge of faith that was distinctively theirs, and could not always be hidden when undressed. There was thus no incentive for uncircumcised Christians, by far the majority by Hadrian's time, to transfer their main day of worship from Saturday to Sunday as a mark of difference from Jews, when their gentle gentile genitals were plain for all to see at Roman communal baths, public toilets, and gymnasia.

---

97. Schäfer, *History of the Jews*, 164; Smallwood *Jews under Roman Rule* 470.
98. Smallwood, *Jews under Roman Rule*, 470.
99. Justin, *Dialogue* 8, 10, 46.
100. Ibid., 19, 23.
101. Ibid., 16, 21.
102. Smallwood, *Jews under Roman Rule* p. 471.

12

The Jewish-Roman War of AD 66–70

The latest Sabbatarian argument to come to my attention is that post-apostolic Christians changed their chief day of worship to Sunday to escape being mistaken for Jews, when the Romans were consolidating their affairs in Judea after the revolt of AD 66–70. This assertion posits that the avenging Roman authorities persecuted Jews, much like some Sabbatarians allege they did after the Bar-Kokhba Revolt. One problem with this argument is that neither Josephus' account,[1] nor that of Eusebius,[2] averts to any thoroughgoing or systematic ethnic cleansing of Jews in Judea, much less in the Diaspora. In fact, Josephus records that the same General Titus who had captured Jerusalem prevented citizens of Antioch-in-Syria from oppressing Jews there.[3] From original research, Eusebius noted that all bishops of Jerusalem and "their whole church consisted then of believing Hebrews" from the era of James the Just until that of Hadrian.[4] This is the opposite of what would be expected if the circumcised had been deported from Judea or forbidden to live there since AD 70. As mentioned

1. Josephus, *Jewish Wars* Book 7.
2. Eusebius, *Church History* 3.5–11.
3. Josephus, *Jewish Wars* 7.5.2.
4. Eusebius, *Church History* 4.5.2, 4.

The Jewish-Roman War of AD 66–70

above under the subheading "The Roman government before AD 135 already distinguished between Judaism and Christianity as separate religions," Judaism was legal and protected under Roman law. This dated from the time of Julius Caesar, that is, before the birth of Jesus, and was confirmed by emperors in 1 BC[5] and AD 41.[6] The Jews thrived unmolested in the Roman Empire before and after AD 70, and were cohesive and strong enough in Judea to sustain an armed uprising from AD 132 to 135. Nor would the large community in Babylonia, outside the Empire, be inclined to break their Sabbath tradition when they were at full liberty to continue it. Sunday-keeping cannot thus be connected to the Roman victory in either revolt.

I doubt that many Sabbatarians are unreflecting enough to accept this argument, because it would work mischief with their other practices and beliefs. Most Sabbatarians consider a change of Christian public worship from Saturday to Sunday as a mark of apostasy and a grave departure from the apostolic order, with the practical consequence that Christian writings after this change are unreliable or outright false, and of no precedent value for Christians today.

If a first-day Lord's Day marks the end of reliability of early Christian literature, what about the parts of the New Testament that were written after AD 70, and the orthodoxy of apostles who lived after it? Advocates of worshipping on the first day of the week call it "the Lord's Day" to distinguish it from the Saturday Sabbath. This is the phrase John used in Revelation 1.10, writing in the AD 90s. If Jesus commanded Christians to worship on the Sabbath, did John deviate from his Lord by observing a day that other early Christian authors used to designate only the first day of the week? Of course, if Christian practices and writings after AD 70 are to be rejected as apostate, we must excise at least the writings of the Apostle John and 2 Peter from the Bible, and find precise dates for

---

5. Augustus, in Josephus, *Antiquities*, 16.6.2; http://legacy.fordham.edu/halsall/ancient/roman-jews.asp#Edict.

6. Claudius, in Josephus, *Antiquities*, 19.5.3; http://legacy.fordham.edu/halsall/ancient/roman-jews.asp#Edict.

the Pastoral Epistles and other New Testament books many church historians and scripture scholars date after AD 70.

Sometimes people ask me "How old is the Christian practice of worshipping on Sunday?" I reply, "Apostolic, if not earlier." In keeping with this, Sabbatarians might be correct when they say it began in AD 70, if they also maintain that the apostles who survived to this time were all apostates.

13

Samuele Bacchiocchi

I suppose I would be remiss if I did not comment on Samuele Bacchiocchi, both his published writings and statements on Youtube.

Rather than engaging in an ecumenical dialogue or producing a balanced, neutral, study, Rev. Bacchiocchi told the examining board of the Gregorian University exactly what it wanted to hear, which was diametrically opposite on a point contested for centuries by other Protestants: the Church of Rome had been supreme in Christendom since its earliest centuries, and the popes possessed from ancient times the same powers as has been official Roman Catholic dogma about them since the First Vatican Council in 1870. Indeed, I have encountered no more succinct and cogent an argument for the antiquity and extent of papal powers, not even in Roman Catholic authors, than on pages 207 to 211 of Bacchiocchi's *From Sabbath to Sunday: A Historical Investigation of the Rise of Sunday Observance in Early Christianity*. In reaching this proposition, Bacchiocchi reiterated the only point that for over a century Roman Catholic writers were in agreement with Seventh-day Adventists, and rejected by Christendom's other Sunday-keepers.

However, the book Bacchiocchi's successor distributes is not the dissertation accepted by the Gregorian for Samuele's doctorate.[1] In the present state of the circulating text, readers do no know how much Sabbatarianism was introduced between the original and present editions. The present pamphlet will consider only the form now distributed by the Bacchiocchis, and his Youtube appearances.

Professor Bacchiocchi quotes or cites a hodgepodge of authors so wide and varied and from so many time periods that any proposition at all can be proved by this method; my comment is that a method that can prove anything proves nothing. He interlaces ancient, medieval, and modern sources as if they were equally contemporaneous witnesses to the antiquities under consideration. There is little, although some, consideration that some sources possess better evidentiary value than other sources, due to difference in time, geographical, cultural, and ideological closeness between the writer and the events and currents under consideration. He even allows the mere opinions and speculations to trump the first-hand evidence of ancient sources. This reminds me of a book by a Roman Catholic who wrote himself into a corner when his discussion of ancient Christian writings teetered on proving a proposition directly contrary to the official position of the Church of Rome today. At the end of his treatise, he noted that Scripture and early church fathers were guided by the Holy Spirit; next, he asserted that the Second Vatican Council was also guided by the same Spirit, which made the Council's decrees more authoritative than what he had worked out in his exposition of early Christian material.

Bacchiocchi cites some authors as proof when he can use them to support of point he favors, only to dismiss them as erroneous or of inferior authority when they wrote contrary to his thesis on another point. He relies so overmuch on what sources do not say that he builds arguments from silence, and misconstrues absence of evidence as evidence of absence. He presents sweeping assumptions as if they were established fact instead of as the very issues it is the purpose of his dissertation to prove. He similarly and subtly introduces speculations and assumptions as fact. His

1. Bacchiocchi, *From Sabbath to Sunday*, 15.

arguments attribute early forces and events to conditions and actions that did not come into existence until centuries later.

Despite sound evidence to the contrary, Bacchiocchi portrays early Roman Christians as so anti-Judaic that they changed their day of worship out of spite and to show that they were not the same as the older religion. He fails to apply the same method of argument to other aspects of Judaism that early proto-catholics retained: belief in a single god, fasts, the Hebrew Bible, weekly communal meetings, philanthropy to the poor and each other, and abstinence from eating or drinking blood. If proto-catholics were as fanatically anti-Judaic as some Sabbatarians believe, we should expect them to have rejected some of these as well. Indeed, the heretical Marcionites rejected the Jewish Bible, and urged other Christians to do the same, but the majority of Christendom accepted and still accepts it.

Youtube gives the impression that Mr. Bacchiocchi (as he then was) made an astounding discovery in the Vatican Library, like a long lost manuscript, and made a significant contribution to twentieth-century scholarship. The material he "discovered" was a section in a book that narrates that the Nazoraeans, a Jewish-Christian denomination, had fled Jerusalem in AD 70 and still kept the Sabbath around AD 350. Making sheer assumptions that Nazoraeans represented a pristine apostolic Christianity, Bacchiocchi tenders this conjecture as evidence that the Jerusalem church kept a seventh-day Sabbath instead of the first day of the week, that this was the universal practice before AD 70, and that Sunday Lord's Day observance began somewhere else—most likely the purportedly anti-Jewish City of Rome.

The facts do not support this impression. Mr. Bacchiocchi discovered nothing new. He merely came across a printed translation of the *Panarion* by the church father Epiphianus, which had already been known for a long time. For example, four translations into Latin had been published before Bacchiocchi was born. A new three-volume critical edition of the original Greek text was published by J. C. Hinrichs at Leipzig between 1915 and 1933, under the editorship of Karl Holl. Bacchiocchi did not unearth a previously unknown manuscript, like the Dead Sea Scrolls or Nag Hammadi library.

When we read the next chapter of the *Panarion*, we find other Jewish-Christians who fled after the fall of Jerusalem, to the same localities as the Nazoraeans,[2] with whom they had once been connected but had separated by the time of Epiphanius.[3] Like them, they observed the Law of Moses, including the Sabbath and, especially, circumcision.[4] Also like them, they rejected all written gospels except that of Matthew.[5] Called Ebionites,[6] they were more faithful followers of the Law than Nazoraeans, in that they avoided touching a Gentile and constantly performed ritual ablutions.[7] Ebionites denied the Virgin Birth,[8] and replaced wine with water in Holy Communion. They were vegetarians,[9] which would make them more similar than the Nazoraeans to Seventh-day Adventists, whom Bacchiocchi identifies as spiritual models and present descendants of the first-century church. Citing Chapter 30 of the *Panarion*, which describes this Ebionite feature, would make a stronger case for Adventism than Chapter 29 and the Nazoraeans, but Bacchiocchi is silent on something a Roman Catholic university would balk at. He himself gave no reason for preferring Nazoraeans to Ebionities, even though they were very similar and found next to each other in the same early sourcebook. Epiphanius also wrote that they were also similar in that they "emulated each other in malice."[10]

As for Nazoraeans, or Ebionites, representing a pre-AD 70 Christian unanimity on the Sabbath vs. Lord's Day practice, they were not the only spiritual descendants of the earliest Jerusalem

2. Epiphanius, Panarion 30.2.7.
3. Epiphanius, Panarion 30.2.8.
4. Epiphanius, Panarion 30.2.2, 30.17.5, 30.26.1–2, 33.3.
5. Epiphanius, Panarion 30.3.7, 53.1.3.
6. Epiphanius, Panarion 30.1.1.
7. Epiphanius, Panarion 30.2.3–5, 30.21.1–2.
8. Epiphanius, Panarion 30.2.2, 30.3.1, 30.16.3.
9. Epiphanius, Panarion 30.15.3, 30.22.1.
10. Epiphanius, Panarion 30.2.9, trans. Williams, 132.

church. It continued in its home city, largely or completely of people of Jewish extraction, until Hadrian expelled them after the Bar-Kokhba Revolt. As other parts of the present pamphlet show, the Christian norm before then was public worship on Sunday, and perhaps a Jewish-like day of rest on Saturday. In fact, all Christianity began at Jerusalem, with the result that even the variants—ancient and modern—are its descendants. Even the church centered in the City of Rome claims to have been founded by two Jews, Peter and Paul. There is no reason to assume that the tiny communities in Syria, Bashan, and Decapolis inhabited by Saturday-keepers kept the primitive Christian praxis in isolation from the vast majority who fellowshipped with apostles that lived after AD 70 and kept Sunday.

Another Nazoraean difference from majority Christianity is indicated in the same passages of the *Panarion* on which Bacchiocchi relies, although he does not deal with it as a weakness in his thesis. According to *Panarion* 29.5.4, 29.7.5, and 29.8.1, the Nazoraeans also practiced circumcision as part of the gospel, putting them at odds with the Jerusalem Council in Acts 15 and Paul's epistles. It is more plausible to believe that Nazoraeans and Ebionites re-introduced the Sabbath and circumcision after AD 70 than that the Jerusalem Council, Paul, and most early and modern Christians throughout the world, became apostate at an early date. Not even Prof. Bacchiocchi's Seventh-day Adventist Church insists on circumcision as a requirement of conversion.

Mr. Bacchiocchi and Prof. Vincenzo Monachno S.J. thought Epiphanius' record was significant as illustrating that any liturgical transfer from Saturday to Sunday did not begin in Jerusalem, but identified the City of Rome as the place of origin. Chapters 2 and 5 through 8 of the present booklet illustrate that Sunday observance was well established in so many places and at so early a date that Rome could not have gradually pressed the "change" over the known world in so short a time. There is no reason to conclusively identify any single point of origin, other than Jesus or the apostles.

If Acts 20.7 and 1 Corinthians 16.2 be any indication (which Bacchiocchi denies), the first records of Christian corporate worship on Sunday come from the watershed of the Aegean Sea. In addition, Sabbatarian and Roman Catholic literature make much of Canon 29 of the Synod of Laodicea-in-Phrygia, which is also in the Aegean basin. If anyone wishes to press the point (which I do not), Sunday observance began in this area, not Rome or Jerusalem. I mention this only to show that Bacchiocchi's methodology in selectivity and juxtaposing of sources, regardless of date or other relationship, can prove anything. Again, the method that can prove anything proves nothing.

Neither the Lukan Acts or the *Panarion* state that the Jerusalem church, the Nazoraeans, or the Ebionites kept the Lord's Day Sunday in addition to the Sabbath. On the other hand, the same writings do not say Christian public worship included Scripture readings, congregational singing, shaking hands, or announcements. In contrast to the Ebionites,[11] Epiphanius does not state that Nazoraeans baptized or celebrated the Eucharist,[12] although there is abundant direct evidence that the New Testament church did. If we are to accept every absence of evidence as evidence of absence, and infer that every silence proves the contrary position, we reach a hermeneutic that is patently unworkable, being capable of supporting any proposition at all, or its contrary. I submit that this is a significant failing of Bacchiocchi and kindred Sabbatarians. I deny that scholars are free to cherry-pick from incompatible inferences in the same ancient author, or assume what they did not imply.

---

11. Epiphanius, Panarion 30.2.4–5, 30.21.1–2.
12. Epiphanius, Panarion 30.16.1.

# 14

Confusion Is Only Apparent

Keeping a Saturday Sabbath does not necessarily preclude public religious observances on the following day. The phenomenon can be observed in our own time in adolescents who do not do their school homework on Saturday, but leave it until late Sunday, and attend a church youth group on the Lord's Day. They do not do this out of religious conscience, for the New Testament nowhere condemns working on a Saturday Sabbath. Yes, despite all the moral injunctions in it (some of them duplicating the other nine Mosaic Commandments), the New Testament neither endorses sabbath-keeping nor prohibits sabbath-breaking.

In fact, neither Old nor New Testament explicitly names which day of the week is the main one for public worship, whether Saturday or Sunday. Sabbatarians choose Saturday because of the Jewish calendar, a source outside the Scriptures. The Jews could have made a mistake in identifying Saturday as the Sabbath, just as they were incorrect in their treatment of Jesus and the apostles, which was at the instigation of their clergy and religious scholars.

15

Conclusion

As illustrated in Acts 20.7, 1 Corinthians 16.2, Didache 14.1, and a large number of other early Christian writings, the main day of the week for Christian public assembly and worship was the Sunday Lord's Day rather than the Saturday Sabbath, the corresponding day in the Jewish religion. Jews also observed it as a day of rest from work, a practice not required of the Christian Sunday until the time of Constantine in the fourth century. This is a point of confusion for Christian Sabbatarians, for they interpret it as a day of both worship and rest, the latter not being the case of majority Christians in the earliest centuries. They performed secular tasks then without conscientious objection. The evidence from sources before the middle of the third century is overwhelming that Christians occupied their weekends in this manner.

The claim that the Roman Catholic Church instituted Sunday as the chief day of worship is vastly overdrawn. The Roman Catholic churchmen whom Sabbatarians quote were motivated by their agenda to persuade Sunday-keeping Protestants into conforming to other observances of the Roman Church, for the sake of consistency, including submission to the pope. In reality, the institution of Sunday Lord's Day is so ancient that it predates the characteristics now associated with the Roman church. Any

Conclusion

change from Saturday to Sunday was apostolic, if not earlier, and could have happened under the aegis of Rome only if the apostles themselves were Roman Catholics. Actually, the papal organization is only one denomination among many descended from the apostolic church, as are Nazoraeans and the denominations listed in the "Introduction" of this booklet.

As demonstrated by the most up-to-date scholarship, early Christians had absolutely no motive for worshipping on Sunday to distinguish themselves from Jews in the eyes of the government. Christians were persecuted for their own religion as early as the Emperor Nero in AD 64, and the Roman government before Constantine regarded the two faiths as separate and distinct. In any event, the only persecution of Jews lasted a mere three years and was confined to Judea. If anything, adherents of the newer religion had more motive to meet on the Saturday Sabbath, so the government would mistake them for Jews, so that Christians would have better chances of being covered by official tolerance of the older religion.

To prevent reliance on dubious allegations of Christian Sunday-keepers, the present pamphlet draws its information from the most accepted Jewish and pagan sources. Such writers had no agenda in the Sabbath/Sunday debate, and were not trying to encourage or forbid any particular Christian religious observances on weekends. I similarly rely on only the most cogent of ancient Christian sources.

Bibliography
The Sources

A reference to an early Christian writer may look impressive, and more so a quotation from one. But how do you know whether the writer of the present pamphlet—or any other author on the subject—copied the original sources correctly and did not take ancient material out of context? This is of particular application for modern writers that mistreat Socrates Scholasticus and Sozomen to make them appear to support a position they never intended.

Following is a bibliography of where you can find some translations of the ancient sources and modern-day information and check on the contexts and accuracy of citations. It includes a list of translations of ancient sources I used, but if you cannot locate them, you should look for other translations. *Barnabas*, *First Clement*, Clement of Alexandria, the *Didache*, the *Letter to Diognetus*, Ignatius, Irenaeus, and Tertullian appear in other translations as well. Some of the older translations are available on the internet, e.g. *The Ante-Nicene Fathers* (ANF), *Nicene and Post-Nicene Fathers of the Christian Church* (NPNF), the *Didascalia*, and Hippolytus's *Apostolic Tradition*. For twentieth-and twenty-first-century authors, the word "In" following double quotation marks indicates that the listed item is an essay that is part of a collection in a book. Do not look under the name of the author of the essay, but the editor of the book. In authors in both eras, the title of the collection is in *italics*.

Bibliography

The internet also contains the catalogues of all libraries likely to stock the books mentioned. If you do not know how to access them, ask for directions at your local library.

Unless you reside in a major metropolis or in a college town, you will probably not find any of the items in the bibliography at a public library. Seminary and university libraries are usually generous in issuing borrower privileges to members of the general public. They usually charge an annual fee for them. If the ones near you do not allow off-campus borrowing, go to your public library and ask for what is called an "interlibrary loan", and show the attendant the items in this bibliography you wish to borrow. Your public library will then borrow the book(s) for you. The library that owns the book might or might not ask for a small fee. Outside Canada and some other countries, you may also need to pay to ship the book(s) between libraries. Check ahead at the public library; the service might well be free of charge in your locality.

Many items in the following bibliography are found only in collections with other short writings. Thus, for anything designated "ANF" in the bibliography, you should ask for the relevant volumes of the *Ante-Nicene Fathers* edited by Roberts and Donaldson. Similarly, ask for Montague Rhodes James'/J. K. Elliott's *The Apocryphal New Testament* rather than *The Epistle of the Apostles* or *Acts of Peter*, for Karlfried Froehlich's *Biblical Interpretation in the Early Church* instead of Ptolemy's *Letter to Flora*, and Schneemelcher's *New Testament Apocrypha* rather than *The Gospel of Thomas*.

Additional information on early writers can be found in the "Guide to Authors and Works Cited in the Lists" at volume 1 pages 121 to 132 of my *Traditional Christian Ethics* (2014). A list of translations is available at pages 163 to 182 of the same volume.

The following bibliography includes a rare feature regarding modern-day authors, which I hope will become standard in the literature. Often while reading, I ask myself: "Does this writer know more than I already do about the subject?" "What are the author's qualifications to write in this field?" "What access does he have to periodicals, ancient writings, current books, and colleagues with whom to discuss the issues, that I do not?" Too often, unscholarly

Bibliography

writers express as "facts" mere half-researched opinions, off the top of their heads, or rely on earlier treatises that have since become outdated or discredited, or on assumptions based on hearsay. Therefore, at the end of each item for a modern author in the bibliography, I indicate their academic credentials. Such addition should greatly assist readers of the present pamphlet in assessing the authors' competence in research, their access to primary or unpublished sources, and how knowledgeable and reliable they are, as against other writers and speakers in the field.

ANF = *The Ante-Nicene Fathers; Translations of The Writings of the Fathers down to A.D. 325*. Edited by Alexander Roberts and James Donaldson. American reprint ed. by A. Cleveland Coxe. Buffalo, NY: Christian Literature Publishing Co., 1885-96; continuously reprinted Grand Rapids, MI: Eerdmans; Peabody, MA: Hendrickson.

NPNF 2d ser. = *Nicene and Post-Nicene Fathers of the Christian Church* Second Series. New York: Christian Literature Publishing Co.; Oxford and London: Parker, 1890; continuously reprinted Edinburgh: T& T Clark; Grand Rapids, MI: Eerdmans; Peabody, MA: Hendrickson.

All references to the Talmud are from the Babylonian Talmud, there being no English or French translation of the Jerusalem Talmud suitable for the purposes of this booklet.

Abusch, Ra'anan. "Negotiating the Difference: Genital Mutilation in Roman Slave Law and the History of the Bar Kokhba Revolt". In *The Bar Kokhba War Reconsidered: New Perspectives on the Second Jewish Revolt against Rome*, edited by Peter Schäfer, 71-91. Tübingen: Mohr Siebeck, 2003. Author is of Princeton University.

Alon, Gedaliah. *The Jews in their Land in the Talmudic Age*. Cambridge, MA: Harvard University Press, 1989. © 1980, 1984 Magness Press, Hebrew University. Eminent Israeli historian on the faculty of the Hebrew University.

Ammianus Marcellinus. *Roman History*, third quarter of fourth century, by a pagan soldier.

Apostles, Epistle of the, sometime between AD 140 and 160. In *The Apocryphal New Testament*. Edited and translated by Montague Rhodes James, 485-503. Oxford: Clarendon, 1953, later reprinted.

Appian. *Roman History: Syrian Wars*. Wrote before AD 162. Translated by Horace White. Cambridge, MA: Harvard University Press; London: Heinemann, 1912-13. Author was a lawyer and public servant.

Bibliography

Aristides. *Apology*. Greece, circa AD 125. ANF 10:[263]–279 in Eerdmans reprint, 9:[263]–79 in Hendrickson reprint.

Aristo of Pella, mid-second century ANF 8:750. In Eusebius, *Church History of Eusebius* 4.6.3. Translated by Arthur Cushman McGiffert, NPNF 1:177. New York: Christian Literature Co.; Oxford: Parker, 1890; continuously reprinted Grand Rapids, MI: Eerdmans; Edinburgh: T & T Clark; Peabody, MA: Hendrickson.

Babylonian Talmud. English translation edited by Isidore Epstein. London: Soncino, 1947. www.Halakhah.com.

Bacchiocchi, Samuele. *Anti-Judaism and the Origin of Sunday: An Excerpt from the Doctoral Dissertation*. Rome: Pontifical Gregorian University Press, 1975.

Bacchiocchi, Samuele. *From Sabbath to Sunday: A Historical Investigation of the Rise of Sunday Observance in Early Christianity*. Rome?: Pontifical Gregorian University Press?, 1977?

Bardesan. *De Fato*, also titled *Book of the Laws of Regions*, written before his death in AD 222/223. ANF 8:723–34.

Barnabas, Letter of, between AD 70 and 132. ANF 1:137–49.

Becker, Adam H. "Christian Society." In *Oxford Handbook of Social Relations in the Roman World*, edited by Michael Peachin, [567]–86. Oxford; New York: Oxford University Press, 2011. Associate Professor of Religious Studies, New York University.

1 *Clement*, between AD 70 and 97. ANF 1:[5]–21, 10:[229]–48.

Clement of Alexandria. *Paedagogus*. Egypt, between AD 192 and 202.

All but Chapter 2.10: ANF 2:209–96.

Chapter 2.10: *Clement of Alexandria: Christ the Educator*. Translated by Simon P. Wood. 164–78. New York: Fathers of the Church, 1954.

———. *Stromata*. between AD 192 and 202.

All but Book 3: ANF 2:299–567.

Book 3: *Alexandrian Christianity: Selected Translations* by John Ernest Leonard Oulton and Henry Chadwick, 40–92. London: SCM; Philadelphia: Westminster Press, 1954.

Constitutio Antoniniana De Civitate peregrinis danda. Edict of the Emperor Caracalla in AD 212 giving Roman citizenship to all free men in the Empire, regardless of ethnicity.

Cyprian. *Dress of Virgins*. Bishop of Carthage, before AD 250. ANF 5:430–36.

Didache, late first century or early second century AD. ANF 7:377–82.

Didascalia apostolorum; The Syriac Version Translated and Accompanied by the Verona Latin Fragments. First three decades of third century AD. Translated by R. Hugh Connolly. Oxford: Clarendon, 1929.

Dio Cassius. *Roman History*. Died AD 235. Translated by Earnest Carey. London: William Heinemann; New York: Macmillan, 1914. Author was a senator and the governor of several Roman provinces.

Diognetus, Letter to, late second century or early third century AD. ANF 1:25–30.

Bibliography

Eliav, Yaron Z. "Jews and Judaism 70–429 C.E." In *A Companion to the Roman Empire*, edited by David S. Potter, [565]–86. Chichester, West Sussex: Wiley-Blackwell, 2010. Assistant Professor of Rabbinic Literature and Jewish History of Late Antiquity in the Department of Near Eastern Studies at the University of Michigan.

Epiphanius of Salamis. *The Panarion of Epiphanius*. Book I. Sects 1–46. Translated by Frank Williams. 2nd ed. Nag Hammadi and Manichaean studies, 63. Leiden, Netherlands: Brill NV, 2009. Written AD 374 to 378.

Eusebius, *Church History of Eusebius*. Written circa AD 325. Translated by Arthur Cushman McGiffert. NPNF 2nd 1.

Everitt, Anthony. *Hadrian and the Triumph of Rome*. New York: Random House, 2009. © 2009 Anthony Everitt. Author is Secretary of the Arts Council for Great Britain.

Fagan, Garrett G. "Leisure." In *A Companion to the Roman Empire*, edited by David S. Potter, [369]–84. Chichester, West Sussex: Wiley-Blackwell, 2010. Associate Professor of Classics and Ancient Mediterranean Studies and History at Pennsylvania State University.

———. "Socializing at the Baths." In *The Oxford Handbook of Social Relations in the Roman World,* edited by Michael Peachin, [358]–73. Oxford: Oxford University Press, 2011.

Flesseman-Van Leer, Ellen. *Tradition and Scripture in the Early Church*. Assen, Netherlands: Van Gorckum, 1954. Freelance Protestant preacher and theological writer who held a Ph.D. but was denied appointments to official church office and university faculties because it was considered inappropriate that such posts be filled by a housewife.

Fredriksen, Paula. "Christians in the Roman Empire in the First Three Centuries CE." In *A Companion to the Roman Empire*, edited by David S. Potter, [587]–606. Chichester, West Sussex: Wiley-Blackwell, 2010. Professor of the Appreciation of Scripture, Social and Intellectual History of Early Christianity in the Department of Religion at Boston University.

Goodblatt, David. "From History to Story to History: the Rimmon Valley Seven." In *The Talmud Yerushalmi and Graeco-Roman Culture,* edited by Peter Schäfer, 1:[173]–99. Tübingen: Mohr Siebeck, 1998. Professor of History at the University of California, San Diego, specializing in the history of the Jewish people, Judaism and the Middle East in the millennium preceding the rise of Islam.

Goodman, Martin. *Rome and Jerusalem*: *The Clash of Ancient Civilizations*. New York: Vintage Books, 2008. © 2007 Martin Goodman. Professor of Jewish Studies at Oxford University.

Hadrian. *Rescript to Caius Minucius Fundanus*. Translated in a supplement to Justin Martyr 1 *Apology* ANF 1:186. Another translation in *A New Eusebius: Documents illustrating the History of the Church to AD 337*, edited by James Stevenson, revised by William H. C. Frend. London: SPCK, 1987, 21–2; a third translation in Eusebius, *Church History* 4.9 NPNF 2d series 1:182. Author was Emperor of Rome. AD 125.

Bibliography

Halsall, Paul, ed. "Ancient History Sourcebook: Roman Sources on the Jews and Judaism, 1 BCE–110 CE." In *Internet Ancient History Sourcebook*, Internet History Sourcebooks Project. http://legacy.fordham.edu/halsall/ancient/roman-jews.asp#Edict. History professor.

Herr, Moshe David. "Persecutions and Martyrdom in Hadrian's Days" *Scripta Hierosolymitana* 6. 1972, [85]–125. Jerusalem: Magness Press, Hebrew University, 1972. Chapter from a doctoral dissertation. Professor of Jewish History, University of Jerusalem.

Hippolytus. *Apostolic Tradition,* AD 217. Translated by Burton Scott Easton *The Apostolic Tradition of Hippolytus.* New York: Macmillan; Cambridge, England: University Press, 1934.

———. *Philosophumena* = *Refutation of All Heresies* 1–2, 4–10, between AD 222 and 235. ANF 5:9–153.

Ignatius of Antioch. *Letter to the Magnesians,* shortly before AD 107. ANF 1:59–65.

Irenaeus of Lyons. *Against Heresies,* AD 180s. ANF 1:315–567.

Josephus. *Antiquities of the Jews.*

———. *Jewish Wars.*

Justin Martyr. *Dialogue with Trypho,* mid-second century AD. ANF 1:194–270.

———. *First Apology,* mid-second century AD. ANF 1:161–87.

———. *Second Apology,* mid-second century AD. ANF 1:188–93.

Kalmin, Richard. "Problems in the Use of the Babylonian Talmud for the History of Late-Roman Palestine: The Example of Astrology." In *Rabbinic Texts and the History of Late-Roman Palestine.* Proceedings of the British Academy 165. 2007, edited by Philip S. Alexander and Martin Goodman, 165-83. Oxford: Oxford University Press for the British Academy, 2010. Professor of Rabbinic Literature at Jewish Theological Seminary of America.

Lavee, Moshe. "Rabbinic Literature and the History of Judaism in Late Antiquity: Challenges, Methodologies and New Approaches." In *Rabbinic Texts and the History of Late-Roman Palestine.* Proceedings of the British Academy 165. 2007, edited by Philip S. Alexander and Martin Goodman, 319–51. Oxford: Oxford University Press for the British Academy, 2007. Lecturer in Talmud and Midrash at University of Haifa.

Leaney, A. R. C. *The Jewish and Christian World 200 BC to AD 200.* Cambridge, UK: Cambridge University Press, 1984. Former Professor of Christian Theology at the University of Nottingham.

Marcus Aurelius. *Meditations,* between AD 170 and 180.

Martial. *Epigrams,* between AD 38/41 and AD 102/104. Translated by Walter C. A. Ker. London: William Heinemann; New York: G. Putnam's Sons, 1925.

Martyrdom of Justin and Companions, circa AD 165. ANF 1:305–6.

Martyrdom of Polycarp, circa AD 136. ANF 1:39–44.

McHugh, Michael. "Marcus Aurelius". In *Encyclopedia of Early Christianity,* edited by Everett Ferguson, 570–1. New York: Garland, 1990. Author is of the University of Connecticut.

Bibliography

Midrash on Psalms. Translated by William G. Braude. New Haven: Yale University Press, 1959.

Midrash Rabbah. Edited by H. Freedman and M. Simon 3rd ed. London: Soncino, 1983. English translation © Soncino, 1983.

Oppenheimer, Aharon. "The Attempt of Hananiah, Son of Rabbi Joshua's Brother, to Intercalate the Year in Babylonia: A Comparison of the Traditions in the Jerusalem and Babylonian Talmuds." In *The Talmud Yerushalmi and Graeco-Roman Culture,* edited by Peter Schäfer and Catherine Hezser, 2:[255]–63. Tübingen: Mohr Siebeck, 2002. © 1998–2002 J. C. B. Mohr (Paul Siebeck). Professor Emeritus of the History of Israel and the Talmud at Tel Aviv University.

Origen, *Commentary on Romans,* between AD 239 and 245:
Translated by Jean Scherer *Le Commentaire d'Origène sur l'Epître aux Romains 3.5 à 5.7 d'après les extraits du Papyrus no 88748 du Musée du Caire et les fragments de la Philocalie et du Vaticanus gr. 762.* Le Caire: Institut français d'archéologie orientale, 1957. Series: Institut français d'archéologie orientale. Bibliothèque d'étude t. 27. Critical edition of Volumes Five and Six.
Translated by Thomas P. Scheck *Origen: Commentary on the Epistle to the Romans* 2 vols. Washington, DC: Catholic University of America Press. Books 1–5 2001; Books 6–10 2002.

———. *De Principiis,* between AD 220 and 230. ANF 4:239–382.

———. *Homélies sur Josué.* Translated by Annie Jaubert. Paris: Cerf, 1960.

———. *Homélies sur les Nombres.* Translated by André Méhat. Paris: Cerf, 1951. Sources chrétiennes 29.

———. *Homélies sur S. Luc; Tomes sur Luc.* Translated by Henri Crouzel, François Fournier, and Pierre Périchon. Paris: Cerf, 1962.

———. *Homilies on Exodus,* between AD 238 and 244. In *Origen: Homilies on Genesis and Exodus.* Translated by Ronald E. Heine. Washington, DC: Catholic University of America Press, 1982.

———. *Homilies on Genesis,* between AD 238 and 244. In *Origen: Homilies on Genesis and Exodus.* Translated by Ronald E. Heine. Washington, DC: Catholic University of America Press, 1982.

———. *Homilies on Isaiah,* between AD 239 and 242. In *Isaïe: Origène, Homélies traduites par Jacques Millet, Sermons d' Augustin, d'Eusèbe le Gallican, de saint Bernard, de Rupert de Deutz traduits par Jacqueline Legée et les Carmélites de Mazille* 21–87. [n.p.]: Desclée de Brower, 1983.

———. *Homilies on Joshua,* AD 249–250. Fathers of the Church series v. 105. Translated by Barbara J. Bruce. Edited by Cynthia White. Washington, DC:Catholic University of America Press, © 2002.

———. *Homilies on Luke,* AD 233–234. *Homilies on Luke; Fragments on Luke.* Translated by Joseph T. Lienhard. Fathers of the Church series vol. 94. Washington, DC: Catholic University of America Press, 1996.

Bibliography

———. *Homilies on Numbers*, between AD 244 and 249. Ancient Christian Texts series. Translated by Thomas P. Scheck. Edited by Christopher A. Hall. Downers Grove, IL: IVP Academic, © 2009.

———. *Letter to Africanus* ANF 4:386-92.

Peter, Acts of, between AD 180 and 200 [fragments]. In *The Apocryphal New Testament* edited and translated by Montague Rhodes James. 300-36. Oxford: Clarendon, 1953, later reprinted.

Pliny the Younger. *Letter* 10.96. Circa AD 112. In *A New Eusebius: Documents Illustrating the History of the Church to AD 337*, edited by James Stevenson, revised by William H. C. Frend, 18-20. London: SPCK, 1987. Roman governor of Bithynia (northwestern Turkey).

Ptolemy the Gnostic. *Letter to Flora*, mid-second century AD. In *Biblical Interpretation in the Early Church*. Edited and translated by Karlfried Froehlich, 37-43. Philadelphia: Fortress, 1985.

Sandgren, Leo Duprée. *Vines Intertwined: A History of Jews and Christians from the Babylonian Exile to the Advent of Islam*. Peabody, MA: Hendrickson, 2010. Adjunct assistant professor of Judaism, Christian origins, and historical fiction at the University of Florida, and holds a Ph.D. in ancient Mediterranean religions. © 2010 Hendrickson Publishers Marketing LLC.

Schäfer, Peter. *The History of the Jews in Antiquity: The Jews of Palestine from Alexander the Great to the Arab Conquest*. New York: Harwood Academic, 1995. Professor of Jewish Studies and Professor of Religion at Princeton University. © Harwood Academic Publishers.

Schwartz, Seth. "Ancient Jewish Social Relations." In *The Oxford Handbook of Social Relations in the Roman World*, edited by Michael Peachin, [548]-66. Oxford: Oxford University Press, 2011. Professor of Classical Jewish Civilization, Columbia University.

Smallwood, E. Mary. *The Jews under Roman Rule: from Pompey to Diocletian*. Leiden: Brill, 1976. © 1976 E. J. Brill. Reader in Classics at the Queen's University in Belfast.

Socrates Scholasticus. *Ecclesiastical History*, between AD 438 and 443. NPNF 2d ser. 2:1-178.

Sozomen, *Ecclesiastical History* circa AD 443. NPNF 2d ser. 2:239-427.

Stern, Sacha. "Talmud Yerushalmi." In *Rabbinic Texts and the History of Late-Roman Palestine*. Proceedings of the British Academy 165. 2007, edited by Philip S. Alexander and Martin Goodman, 143-64. Oxford: Oxford University Press for the British Academy, 2010. Professor of Jewish Studies at University College, London. Proceedings of the British Academy 165. 2007. © 2010 The British Academy.

Strack, Hermann L., and Günter G. Stemberger. *Introduction to the Talmud and Midrash*. Translated by Marcus Bockmuehl. Edinburgh: T & T Clark, 1991. Translation of *Einleitung in Talmud und Midrash*. Strack was a Protestant orientalist who died in 1922; Stemberger is Professor Emeritus of Jewish Studies at the University of Vienna active in the late twentieth century and twenty-first century.

Bibliography

Suetonius. *Lives of the Twelve Caesars*. Written during Hadrian's reign. Translated by John C. Rolfe. London: Heinemann, 1913-14. Loeb Classical Library.
Tacitus. *Annals*. Translated by Alfred John Church and William Jackson Brodribb. London: Macmillan, 1869 reprinted 1906. Another translation in James Stevenson, revised by William H. C. Frend. *A New Eusebius : Documents Illustrating the History of the Church to AD 337*, edited by James Stevenson, revised by William H. C. Frend, 2-3. London: SPCK, 1987. Author was a senator; lived AD 56 to 117.
Tertullian. *Ad Nationes* = *To the Nations*, circa AD 197. ANF 3:[109]-47.
———. *Against Marcion*, between AD 207 and 212. ANF 3:[271]-474.
———. *Answer to the Jews*, between AD 197 and 202. ANF 3:[151]-73.
———. *Apologeticum*, AD 197. ANF 3:[17]-55.
———. *On Fasting*, in his Montanist period. ANF 4:102-14.
———. *On Idolatry*, between AD 208 and 212. ANF 3:[61]-76.
———. *On Modesty*, in his Montanist period. ANF 4:74-101.
Theophilus of Antioch. *To Autolycus*, third quarter of second century AD. ANF 2:89-121.
Thomas, Gospel of, between AD 150 and 200. Translated by Beate Blatz. In *New Testament Apocrypha*, edited by Wilhelm Schneemelcher. English translation by R. McL. Wilson. Revised ed. 1:117-29. Cambridge, UK: James Clarke; Louisville, KY: Westminster/John Knox, 1991.
Toner, J. *Leisure and Ancient Rome*. Cambridge, UK: Polity Press, 1995. Associate of Clare Hall, Cambridge.
Trajan. *Reply to Pliny*. Circa AD 112. In collection of Pliny the Younger *Letter* 10.9.7. In *A New Eusebius: Documents Illustrating the History of the Church to AD 337*, edited by James Stevenson, revised by William H. C. Frend, 20-1. London: SPCK, 1987. Author was Emperor of Rome.
Yegül, Fikret K. *Bathing in the Roman World*. New York: Cambridge University Press, 2010. Professor emeritus of architectural history, University of California at Santa Barbara.

www.ingramcontent.com/pod-product-compliance
Lightning Source LLC
Chambersburg PA
CBHW051702090426
42736CB00013B/2508